KNOWING CHILDREN
Participant Observation with Minors

GARY ALAN FINE
KENT L. SANDSTROM
University of Minnesota

Qualitative Research Methods,
Volume 15

SAGE PUBLICATIONS
The Publishers of Professional Social Science
Newbury Park   Beverly Hills   London   New Delhi

For information address:

SAGE Publications, Inc.
2111 West Hillcrest Drive
Newbury Park, California 91320

SAGE Publications Inc.
275 South Beverly Drive
Beverly Hills
California 90212

SAGE Publications Ltd.
28 Banner Street
London EC1Y 8QE
England

SAGE PUBLICATIONS India Pvt. Ltd.
M-32 Market
Greater Kailash I
New Delhi 110 048 India

Printed in the United States of America

Library of Congress Cataloging-in-Publication Data

Fine, Gary Alan.
    Knowing children : participant observations with minors / Gary
Alan Fine and Kent L. Sandstrom.
        p.   cm. — (Qualitative research methods ; v. 15)
    Bibliography: p.
    ISBN 0-8039-3364-9 :   ISBN 0-8039-3365-7 (pbk.)
        1. Children—Research—Methodology—Case studies.   2. Participant
observation—Case studies.   I. Sandstrom, Kent L.   II. Title.
III. Series.
HQ767.85.F56   1988
305.2′3′072—dc19   88-14016
                                                        CIP

When citing a University Paper, please use the proper form. Remember to cite the correct Sage University Paper series title and include the page number. One of the following formats can be adapted (depending on the style manual used):

(1) KIRK, JEROME and MARC L. MILLER (1986) Reliability and Validity in Qualitative Research. Sage University Paper Series on Qualitative Research Methods, Vol. 1. Beverly Hills, CA: Sage.

or

(2) Kirk, J., & Miller, M. L. (1986). *Reliability and validity in qualitative research* (Sage University Paper Series on Qualitative Research Methods, Vol. 1). Beverly Hills, CA: Sage.

CONTENTS

TO

THE CHILDREN OF THE WORLD

WHO HAVE SUFFERED

AT THE HANDS OF ADULTS

EDITORS' INTRODUCTION

All of us study children. If not our own, certainly those down the block, those portrayed on television, those who come to visit, or those who simply lounge about blocking the entrance to the subway or mall. It could hardly be otherwise for our sense of what it means to be an adult depends in crucial ways on what we think it is (was) like to be a child. Ideology, proximity, concern, and, of course, memory all contribute to what we make of our daily experience with children. While such practical theorizing about children rarely hardens into a formal sort, it does seem the case that most of us probably share the conceit that we understand children at least as well as they understand themselves. Such a conceit is not unlike one carried by cultural snobs everywhere who think of culture as something they have plenty of but others lack.

Gary Alan Fine and Kent L. Sandstrom bring this conceit up short in the 14th volume of the Sage Series on Qualitative Research Methods. By making sharp use of the relevant ethnographic literature, they point out that the cultural worlds created by children are often as inventive, rule-governed, nuanced and guarded as those created by adults. More to the point, perhaps, they also demonstrate just how difficult it is for fieldworkers to penetrate (or be penetrated by) these worlds. In a telling line, Fine and Sandstrom suggest that "discovering what children really know may be as difficult as learning what our pet kitten really thinks . . . we think we can make sense of what behaviors have just occurred, but can we be sure we are not reading into their actions?" This is a knotty problem indeed and spills over into virtually all of contemporary social science.

Not all the issues covered in this book are perched on such an epistemological highwire. *Knowing Children* is full of useful guidelines for those who wish to venture into the child's world as offered by two fieldworkers who have already done so. The double entendre of the title captures well the problematic character of such quests for the children represented in this work are anything but innocent or unknowing when it comes to dealing with inquisitive adults. They are masters of indirection and hard truth, gleeful chicanery and stoic reserve. This is, of course, what makes fieldwork with children trying but it is also what makes it fun.

—John Van Maanen
Peter K. Manning
Marc L. Miller

PREFACE

Few groups in our culture are as close and as distant as are our children. We share a bond (with each other and with them) in that we were children once ourselves. We experienced those changes of age through which they will inexorably pass. We should know our children because we were once like them.

Yet, there is a sense in which we do not know our children very well. While our children do tell us about themselves, they are careful in what they say. Children quickly become masters of impression management and are quite adept in what they reveal (Fine, 1981). Children typically have several groups before which they perform, and they learn that what is permissible with one audience is quite *outré* with another. They also learn that if they can shield their behaviors from adults, then those adults are much less likely to learn about them—and may even believe that these disagreeable behaviors simply do not exist. Although we may spend much time interacting with our children, we do not fully know them. Moreover, we may not even have the desire or ability to understand what they do tell us. As "grownups," we are limited by our tendency to process their talk through our own view of the world. We are constrained by the "adultcentric" (Goode, 1986) nature of our understandings.

This fact suggests the need for observational and in-depth research with children to learn more about their culture. When we are physically distant from groups—such as the traditional tribal cultures that anthropologists have studied—we are typically more aware of our

AUTHORS' NOTE: Some of the material found throughout this monograph was first published in different form in Gary Alan Fine and Barry Glassner, 1979, "Participant Observation With Children: Promise and Problems," *Urban Life* 8(July):153-174; and Gary Alan Fine, 1980, "Cracking Diamonds: Observer Role in Little League Baseball Settings and the Acquisition of Social Competence," in *Fieldwork Experience: Qualitative Approaches to Social Research*, edited by William B. Shaffir, Robert A. Stebbins, and Allan Turowetz, New York: St. Martin's Press. We wish to thank John Van Maanen, Peter Manning, William Corsaro, Peter Adler, and Patricia Adler for their helpful comments.

cultural (or symbolic) distance and so can more easily recognize our differences. We also tend to appreciate better the importance of *their* perspective. When we are studying children, however, we frequently assume that "our" view of the world will be their view (although we may believe that we are more knowledgeable and sophisticated than they are). Such a perspective may cause us to lose the trail of their culture. The challenge of doing qualitative research (for that matter, all research) with children stems from the problems posed by the combination of their *physical* closeness and simultaneous *social* distance. While there is some disagreement among scholars as to how easy it is for adults to gain access to the world of childhood (Waksler, 1986), the assumptions and values of these two social categories inevitably differ.

Throughout this book, we will refer often to the somewhat inchoate concept of children's culture. We use a somewhat casual, behavioral definition (see Fine, 1987), referring to children's talk, behavior, and the public presentation of their beliefs and attitudes. Actually it is better to speak of children's cultures, as children differ greatly by age and circumstance, and, as a consequence, what they know and what they do differs as well.

One frequently hears the lament that not much research has been conducted on children (e.g., Ambert, 1986). Nevertheless, we were impressed in preparing this book by the amount and range of qualitative studies of children that have been conducted in a variety of disciplines (e.g., sociology, anthropology, psychology, education, political science, child development, and even geography). In fact, the number of articles and books published involving qualitative research with children is increasing. This trend is illustrated in the first two volumes of the annual *Sociological Studies of Child Development* (Adler and Adler, 1986, 1987). Although there may never be enough research for a complete understanding of children's worlds, a sufficient body of literature exists to provide us with the basis for generalization. In terms of methodology, various articles and appendixes in monographs have appeared regarding the problems of conducting qualitative research with children. Yet, until this volume, there has been no extended treatment of the methodological problems of qualitative research with children that integrates previous writings. This book is a partial attempt to correct that lacuna.

We shall focus on one style of research: participant observation.[1] While we shall address in passing the problems of conducting in-depth interviews with children[2] (Bierman and Schwartz, 1986; Parker, 1984; Tammivaara and Enright, 1986) and life history research (Shaw, 1930;

Wolcott, 1983), our focus is on studies that use ethnographic techniques. We believe that the issue of how to interview children (and, for that matter, how to conduct archival or ecological research on children's culture) deserves separate treatment elsewhere, although we assume that many of the issues we raise will resonate with other methodologies.

One of the challenges in describing research with *children* derives from the fact that it is difficult if not impossible to discuss the study of children, abstracted from an analysis of their age. It seems ludicrous to discuss techniques for approaching a 2- and a 17-year-old under the same rubric. For this reason, we focus our discussion on three ages of children: (1) preschoolers (4- to 6-year-olds), (2) preadolescents (10- to 12-year-olds), and (3) middle adolescents (14- to 16-year-olds). Given that research does not respect our artificial categories, we shall discuss studies of children of other ages when necessary. We chose to focus on several ages, rather than to cover every age. Other key social factors affecting research with children, such as gender, class, or nationality, will be discussed where germane.

After an introductory chapter exploring some of the general issues involved in research with those under the age of legal consent, we shall devote separate chapters to the problems of conducting participant observation research with each of these groups. We shall focus on one research study for each of these age groups, while not ignoring other research that has been conducted on these groups.

The three case studies that we shall draw upon for the many empirical examples are (1) an ethnography of a nursery school in Berkeley, California, conducted by William Corsaro (1985); (2) an ethnography of ten Little League Baseball teams in five leagues in Massachusetts, Rhode Island, and Minnesota (Fine, 1987); and (3) an 18-month participant observation study of fantasy role-playing gamers (including Dungeons & Dragons) in the Twin Cities (Fine, 1983).

Each of these studies has the advantage of being a detailed examination of the world of American children, conducted over a considerable period of time. The focus in each is on nondeviant middle-class white males—a limitation that should be recalled while reading the book. Corsaro and Fine are middle-class white males themselves, and this limited what they could learn and, no doubt, what they chose to ask. In addition, the last two studies have the advantage of being well known to the senior author, who is painfully aware of the limitations of the methodology and the errors that occurred as the data were being collected. In the ensuing chapters, we shall briefly describe the basic content and methodology of these studies, and then we shall address how they shed light on research efforts with that age group.

We hope that this book will not stand as a final word. Instead, we offer it as a helpful beginning statement upon which others may build or to which they may respond. As we noted earlier, there is increasing interest in research that examines minors. In light of this, it seems essential that our methodological skills keep pace with our empirical observations and theoretical formulations. Without methodological self-reflection, all our findings will be built on mounds of shifting sand; our children deserve better.

The title of this book, *Knowing Children*, carries with it a deliberate double entendre. Perhaps the most obvious goal of qualitative research with children is to get to know them and better to see the world through their eyes. On a deeper level, this style of research additionally assumes that minors are knowledgeable about their worlds, that these worlds are special and noteworthy, and that we as adults can benefit by viewing the world through their hearts and minds.

NOTES

1. Although most readers of this book will have considerable knowledge of what participant observation research entails, a brief definition is in order. Taylor and Bogdan (1984, p. 15) define participant observation as "research that involves social interaction between the researcher and informants in the milieu of the latter, during which data are systematically and unobtrusively collected." Note that this might involve situations in which the observer is a covert member of the group. For more information on participant observation research, see Spradley (1980), Jackson (1987), Lofland (1976), Schatzman and Strauss (1973), and other volumes in the Sage Qualitative Methods series.

2. Baker (1983) argues that, by interviewing children, one is creating a "real" relationship between the child (in this case, an adolescent) and the adult. The "interview" can be seen as a natural instance of adolescent socialization, edging interviews closer to participant observation.

1. RESEARCHERS AND KIDS

Like the white researcher in black society, the male researcher studying women, or the ethnologist observing a distant tribal culture, the adult participant observer who attempts to understand a children's culture cannot pass unnoticed as a member of that group.[1] The structure of age roles in American society (Davis, 1940; Parsons, 1942) makes impossible the enactment of the complete participant role (Gold, 1958). Patterns of age segregation in American society (Conger, 1971) mean that it is unexpected for an adult to "hang out" with children's groups; legitimate adult-child interaction depends on adult authority. The taken-for-granted character of this authority structure and the different world-views that are related to it create unique problems for participant observation with children. While certain problems are applicable to research with other "protected groups" (e.g., the mentally retarded; Edgerton, 1984), other problems are distinctive because of the effects of the age difference between researcher and informant.

In traditional ethnographic settings, a common assumption is that one's research subjects are equal in status to oneself, or at least should be treated as such. For instance, ethnographers typically treat members of the underclass, criminals, the mentally ill, the sick, or the infirm with the same respect with which they treats their colleagues. While status is always an issue the sensitive researcher examines, the muting of status lines is more common than deepening or reinforcing them. Yet, in participating with children, such a policy is not fully tenable, because the social roles of the participants have been influenced by age, cognitive development, physical maturity, and acquisition of social responsibility.

In this chapter, we shall describe some of the fundamental problems that must be confronted by a researcher studying children of any age. More specifically, we will describe (1) research roles open to adults, (2) ethical implications of the research, (3) techniques for achieving rapport, and (4) general problems involved with understanding children's meanings. Obviously these are issues that emerge in research with adults, but the forms that they take in studying children are significantly different. Underlying this analysis is our claim that "normal" relationships between adult and child in American society must be taken into account in planning research.

Research Roles

Roles that adults assume when they study children may be differentiated on two dimensions: (1) the extent of positive contact between adult and child, and (2) the extent to which the adult has direct authority over the child (Fine and Glassner, 1979). These dimensions are in reality not dichotomous, although, for this discussion, we will treat them as such. The roles presented are ideal types, seldom, if ever, found in practice. While there are many "roles" that characterize the relations that adults have with children, we find these two *dimensions* to be particularly central in depicting the possibilities for research. We do not claim that these role labels are absolute or "real" in any meaningful sense, although we believe that the dimensions that lie behind them seem to us to be characteristic of all contact with children.

It is the authority dimension, in particular, that separates research with adults from research with children. With the exception of some studies of the institutionalized "ill" or "protected" (e.g., Goffman, 1961), adult researchers are not in positions of direct, formal authority over adult informants. Only in research with children can authorities legitimately conduct ethnographic work with their charges. Although we shall focus on the role of the friend (positive affect and low authority) in this book, we are not setting up the other roles as "straw men." They are legitimate research techniques, although, in their more extreme form, they pose problems different from the friend role.

SUPERVISOR

In its pure form, the supervisor role (authority; no positive affective relations) seems incompatible with ethnographic research. Authorities who do not express positive feelings toward their charges are unlikely to write about their experiences. Such figures include authoritarian teachers, camp supervisors, and religious instructors. Generally this role provides access to a relatively restricted range of youthful behavior. Often in such situations, the child will behave in one way while being observed (and under coercion) and a quite different way when removed from the gaze of an authority. Thus children, particularly by the time they are able to attend school, have developed techniques of impression management that permit them to "get by" in front of disliked or feared authorities in order to avoid disapproval or reprimand. Although the level of dramaturgical skill and information control differs by age, the goal remains constant. The behaviors observed may be "natural," but these observations will only include a small portion of the children's behavior. Within the context of this role, it is unlikely that the barriers between adults and children will be breached.

A research example of the supervisor role (or at least a modified version of the role) is exemplified by a study of sociometric relations in a 10th-grade class (Cook, 1945). The experimenter, after determining the sociometric patterns of the class, decided selectively to alter these social relations to make for a "better" learning environment. Although Greeley and Casey (1963) do not describe the nature of their contact with an upper-middle-class gang, it appears that they manipulated the relations of the group they studied, because they admitted that they presided over the "liquidation" of the gang.

LEADER

The leader can be differentiated from the supervisor by the presence of positive contact with the child, although legitimate authority remains. The leader role is seen most clearly in the many popular treatments of teacher-student contact (e.g., Kohl, 1967; Kozol, 1967; Richmond, 1973). In addition to teachers, other professionals who regularly deal with groups of children adopt this role—camp counselors, coaches, or scout troop leaders. Children have somewhat greater leeway for action in such relationships, and even when they overstep the line of proper behavior, tolerance will frequently be shown by the adult leader. The normative frame of reference, however, remains that of the adult. Children may even feel constrained to be on their "best behavior" so as not to embarrass their leader. Their affection and regard for their leader may prevent them from revealing private feelings or behavior, which may be contrary to the image that they wish to portray. This respect may serve as a barrier for research. The adult, in turn, is expected by his or her charges to behave like an adult. As a leader, he or she can never simply remain in the background and watch how children's culture develops.

OBSERVER

The observer role is the inverse of the leader role. He or she is an adult without formal authority and affective relationships. Indeed, such a role is not consistent with *participant* observation, but it may be used where a record of overt behavior is more important than the rhetorics that children give to explain their behaviors. While children may not consciously behave so as to obtain approval, neither do they admit the observer into their confidences. Children have little or no motivation to allow the observer to learn the social contingencies by which their group operates. Because the observer is seen as an adult, they will hide those behaviors to which they think anonymous adults might object. For instance, preadolescent boys sometimes post a lookout for adults and quickly change the subject when an adult is present. Similarly, when children wish to engage in socially deviant acts, they often retreat to private locations where a stranger cannot follow. The pure observer is granted little more right to witness their behavior than any member of the general public, although this may vary depending upon how the researcher presents the study. Even if the observer witnesses normally "hidden" behavior, its meaning may remain opaque, and the children involved have little incentive to explain it. The meaning of the behavior may only become known (perhaps inaccurately) because of the overlap in shared culture between adult and child.

Being an outsider is difficult. It is natural to wish to establish friendly relations. Polansky and his colleagues (1949) attempted to employ this approach in observing early adolescents in a summer camp for disturbed children. They discovered that the observer role proved threatening to the children, and to some extent to the counselors as well, because of the anxiety involved in being observed without feedback. By the second week of camp, the researchers decided to humanize their role, and subsequently became observer-friends. Glassner encountered similar anxieties during his research at a St. Louis elementary school when he adopted a cross between the observer role and the friend role. He noted occasions when some of his subjects found it uncomfortable to be observed without a full explanation (Glassner, 1976, pp. 19-20). One boy even hid from the researcher and later cried violently about being observed—until he received an explanation of why Glassner was taking notes.

A particularly common type of observation involves watching children in a public area—such as a park, playground, or street. In such locales, one finds adults sitting and standing without providing a public explanation (Polgar, 1976; Dawe, 1934; St. J. Neil, 1976; Sluckin, 1981). These studies provide much behavioral and descriptive data, but often the collection of explanations from the children's point of view is left to others.

FRIEND

The final major type of participant observation role, and the one emphasized in this book, is to become a friend to one's subjects and interact with them in the most trusted way possible—without having any explicit authority role. As indicated above, in our view, this will always be an ideal type because of the demographic and power differences involved. Yet, some researchers emphasize the possibilities of a true equality of friendship between an adult and child (Goode, 1986)—the adoption of the least-adult role (Mandell, 1988).[2] We believe there is methodological value in maintaining the differences between sociologists and children—a feature of interaction that permits the researcher to behave in certain "nonkid" ways—such as asking "ignorant" questions.[3]

To the extent that the researcher can transcend age and authority boundaries, children may provide access to their "hidden" culture (Llewellyn, 1980; Knapp and Knapp, 1976). The friend role is conducive to the development of trust, although this trust must be cultivated by the researcher. As we shall discuss below, children create interpretations of who the researcher is and what he or she wants to know. Children may suspend their typical modes of dealing with adults, but this type of unique interaction takes time to develop. Often children will make note of this relationship (e.g., giving the researcher a nickname), so as to indicate its special nature. This was impressed on the senior author when he was studying preadolescent baseball teams, and one preadolescent labeled him an "honorary kid," to signal to a friend (with whom the senior author did not have a relationship) that they could talk in his presence.

The key to the role of friend is the explicit expression of positive affect combined with both a relative lack of authority and a lack of sanctioning of the behavior of those being studied. In turn, adopting the friend role suggests that the participant observer treats his or her informants with respect and that he or she desires to acquire competency in their social worlds.

Developing the Friend Role

Given that the friend role is the basis of much participant observation, including that with children, how can it be cultivated? We will focus on how this role (and the research associated with it) is explained to children.

To be in any location, one needs a justification, an account for oneself. In much of our lives, these justifications are implicit. We walk on the street because streets are public arenas and we are going somewhere. We attend sports events because we enjoy watching those events and have paid for the right to be present. Of course, some locations call for a greater explanation. If an adult wishes to be present in a sixth-grade classroom, he or she cannot simply walk in and say that it is public space (which it is) or that he or she is interested in what is occurring (although he or she may be). Rather, one must provide gatekeepers of those locations with a credible account of one's presence. Access becomes a more difficult issue in relatively small and privately operated environments that are occupied by protected or deviant groups. On the other hand, access is more taken for granted in large, public places that are populated by a heterogeneous crowd.

Yet, gaining access to a location does not mean that one will become part of a group. Simply to be near children does not mean that one will automatically become their friend. Further explanations are necessary to cultivate a relationship—that is, one needs a justification or "cover" (Fine, 1980, p. 122) for the unexpected social relationship. In nonresearch situations, one may be able to cite the sponsorship of an acquaintance or the existence of some biographical interest that legitimates one's presence. These natural explanations are routinized and conventionalized, and typically are not problematic. In natural interaction,[4] the explanation that is given will often be the one that the explainer privately accepts—it is the *real* reason for the person's presence. Justifications must be accepted both by the group and by the participant. This proffering of justifications may be particularly difficult in settings with several distinct groups of actors, as each group (adult guardians and children) may have their own criteria for acceptance and their own understandings. If the explanations are too much at variance (and are not backed up by appropriate behavior), either group may become suspicious of the researcher.

In response to these dilemmas, three basic approaches have been used by researchers to explain their presence. First, the participant observer may provide the research subjects with a complete and detailed explanation of the purposes and hypotheses of the research; this we term "explicit cover." Second, the researcher may explain that research is being conducted, but be vague or less than completely candid about its goals—"shallow cover." Finally, the researcher may deliberately hide the research from informants—"deep cover."

EXPLICIT COVER

Although an explicit announcement of one's research might at first seem to be the most ethically responsible tactic, it also creates methodological problems. Even when the observer presents his or her role as "objectively" as possible, this does not mean that the children, who lack experience with sociological investigations, will understand this explanation "properly." There is also danger in telling informants too much about one's research goals, and this danger consists of more than the expectancy effect by which knowledgeable subjects attempt to confirm or deny the researcher's hypotheses. The explanation given may, if sufficiently explicit, limit what informants decide to share with their friend. Further, by presenting the research as more formal than it is (considering the flexible nature of grounded research; Glaser and Strauss, 1967), friendships may be less likely. The relationships that develop are likely to be utilitarian ones, based upon the formal research bargain. A good example of how limited research goals can be facilitated by a modified version of explicit cover is an ethnographic study of the social dynamics of a car pool (Adler and Adler, 1984). Here the topic was limited in scope and was not emotionally sensitive. Also, by virtue of being drivers, the researchers had the advantage of having legitimate relations with the informants separate from the research bargain.

SHALLOW COVER

The approach that the senior author used in his own research with Little League baseball players is "shallow cover"—an explanation most notable for its "sin" of omission. While explicitly mentioning and reaffirming that he was a social psychologist interested in observing the behavior of preadolescents, this was not expanded upon in detail. He claimed that he wished to discover what children said and did, and that he would spend as much time with them as possible (see also Cusick, 1973; Llewellyn, 1980; Hollingshead, 1975). This vague bargain permitted informal arrangements with many individuals—explanations that could differ substantially. Some players treated him as an intimate, sharing their dirty stories and vile exploits; others used him as a protector against the bullying of their peers. He also provided isolated boys with someone to talk to about their baseball concerns; and he was an audience for parents and coaches to describe their frustrations in raising children (Fine, 1987).

Shallow cover makes one's structural role explicit, and, as such, the researcher's credibility cannot be undermined. Yet, no matter how vague the researcher attempts to be, children develop ideas of what the researcher is looking for. These ideas can be cruelly or benignly disconfirmed and that disconfirmation may affect the researcher's access to the subjects. Shallow cover is perhaps the most frequent approach and may account for the fact that, occasionally, after a research account is published (Gallagher, 1964; Vidich and Bensman, 1964), informants will feel betrayed when the ambiguous explanation becomes clear in retrospect. Although the informants are not defrauded, in that they knowingly participated in research, the topics of study were not what they expected them to be. For instance, a researcher who is interested in sexism and interpersonal violence might avoid telling informants of this fact, and the publication of his or her conclusions may be traumatic for them.

Using shallow cover, one can create flexible research bargains. Because the researcher may initially have no firm hypotheses (a basis of inductive research), the research problem can be narrowed or shifted while maintaining the original research bargain. Thus, when the senior author expanded his focus from what occurred on baseball diamonds to what preadolescents did in their leisure time, he could successfully do this because it did not violate the original bargain.

DEEP COVER

In research studies in which subjects are unaware that they are being observed, the researcher is operating in a manner analogous to an undercover intelligence agent—although perhaps with a more benign set of motives. Here one may witness a wide variety of behaviors, but may simultaneously find it difficult to inquire about any of these behaviors without arousing suspicion. A cover that is exposed in such a situation—when subjects discover that their new "friend" is actually a sociologist—may have profound implications. The exposure discredits not only the research, but also the researcher.

Deep cover is primarily an issue in research with late adolescents, where some possibility of "passing" can occur. One might also apply this approach, however, to legitimate authorities who are collecting data in their legitimate roles without informing subjects. For example, Muzafer Sherif portrayed a camp custodian in his summer camp studies (Sherif et al., 1961; Sherif and Sherif, 1953), while David Voigt and Lewis Yablonsky were actually coaches when they studied Little League baseball (Voigt, 1974; Yablonsky and Brower, 1979).

This kind of deception, while generally innocuous in its immediate moral consequences, typically can be sustained only for a short period because of (1) the frustrations that affect the researcher, and (2) the limitations that are built into the role in terms of lack of access to the meanings that the events have for participants. While "real" group members may believe that the researcher knows as much about the rules of the game as they do, he or she actually knows less and finds no easy path to discovery.

The research announcement made by the participant observer influences his or her ability to feel comfortable within the setting. Deep cover is clearly the most problematic in that the research is continually in danger of being unmasked. Discrediting or revealing information must be hidden. While explicit cover promotes personal comfort— because little discrepancy exists between public and private roles—a change in the research bargain may cause trouble and the observer must acquire new abilities (such as the ability to talk about preadolescent sexual behavior as well as baseball). The third approach is most conducive to acquiring situational competency. Shallow cover avoids having the research discredited, and, due to the open focus of the researcher's role, it allows for questioning of the rules and appropriate behaviors of the group, both in public and in private.

Building Trust

The nature of participant observation requires that the researcher gains access to settings—particularly those to which he or she would not "normally" have access as a member of the general public. This is achieved through gaining rapport with a group.

Not every researcher is suitable for every research setting. Each observer has strengths and weaknesses, preferences and fears—together these make up the researcher's personal equation. A basic requirement for a participant observer is that he or she emotionally empathizes and doesn't feel excessive personal anxiety becoming close to those being studied (Johnson, 1975). Most individuals are "comfortable" with some groups, and ill at ease with others. While liking is a part of this response, it also connects to the basic—and sometimes unstated and unrecognized—moral, social, or political values of the researcher. The senior author has found working with children exhilarating, although others might find that same research tiresome or anxiety-producing. In order to be a participant observer with children, one must be able to deal with them on a relatively equal footing and one must also have the ability and desire to listen to them. Further, this kind of research requires giving up some of one's adult prerogatives and occasionally shelving some of one's "adult" dignity.

Adults may place themselves in the same location with children, but this does not mean that children will reveal their secrets. Texts on how to conduct participant observation typically recommend that researchers remain passive and nondistracting (Taylor and Bogdan, 1984). Yet, adults are salient individuals in children's social worlds and are difficult to ignore due to the authority that usually accompanies their age. Whatever technique one adopts, the problem of reactivity must not be overlooked and all data collected from children must be examined for artifacts arising from adult presence.

Given these challenges, we argue that there are two general techniques that may be employed to increase rapport and access. The first is for the adult to adopt the behavior and values of the children—essentially having the adult become a "peer," and the second is for the adult to employ social rewards and material gifts to promote acceptance.

SHARED VALUES AND BEHAVIORS

As tempting as it might be, "going native" is simply not viable. Yet, researchers may adopt many of the behaviors of the children and adolescents they study. Hollingshead (1975, p. 15) notes: "We 'ganged' and 'clowned' with the adolescents in their 'night spots' and favorite 'hangouts,' after the game, dance or show." He courteously refrained from observing lover's lanes, however. The senior author attempted to spend as much time with preadolescent baseball players as he could, but they and he felt that it would not be tactful if he were present when "moons were shining,"[5] at boy-girl parties, or when eggs were thrown at neighboring houses. He was, however, told about these events in great detail. He inquired about going with the boys when they played pranks or attended boy-girl parties, but this never happened. The anxiety about his observation of cross-gender contacts or sexual matters can be seen in the comment of a boy who told a player who had invited him to a party,

"He wants to see you screw your girlfriend." Obviously, observation of preadolescent sexuality would involve very sensitive topics that are outside the normal sphere of adult-child interaction.

A fine line exists between what is considered appropriate behavior by the observer and what is awkward for both parties. Although one may wish to obtain as much data as possible to understand the world of these children, one should avoid behaving in ways that make one uncomfortable. Given the differences between acceptable adult and child behavior, this discomfort may occur when the adult strives to be a peer. Most children can sense whether a researcher looks like a good bet as a friend (Cottle, 1973) and will usually spot those who attempt to be something other than what they are and who make them uncomfortable. It was a memorable moment for the senior author when one boy told another about a mutual secret, "You can tell Gary. He's one of the boys." Being "one of the boys" was a mark of acceptance by these preadolescents.

While being approving, sympathetic, and supportive leads to increased rapport, a false attempt to be "with it" may backfire—not only making the researcher feel anxious, but also cutting off research opportunities. Children's slang is hard for an adult to master, and even when learned correctly, often sounds strange when uttered by an adult. (How many researchers can say "poop" or "rad" with a straight face?) Researchers, particularly those studying adolescents, may be offered drink or drugs, either as a test or an act of friendship, and the researcher must decide how to respond (Lowney, 1984). The key point is that intimacy cannot be rushed, and close relationships may never develop if pressured. Many researchers (e.g., Corsaro, 1985; Glassner, 1976; Fine, 1987) describe a period of some weeks in which they were treated as nonpersons before the long—and never-ending—road to acceptance began.

Aside from building trust with the children he or she is studying, a participant observer who lacks formal authority must also negotiate rapport with adult authorities or guardians who are present or who have responsibility for these children. A wise participant observer should carefully cultivate and maintain these relationships to prevent misunderstandings, such as the reaction of parents to one researcher who, as a girl scout leader, was accused of not sufficiently instilling discipline in her troop (E. Tucker, personal communication, 1976). These rapport-building contacts enable one to obtain an informative perspective, while simultaneously ensuring that no objections are being raised to one's actions. This should not affect one's research negatively, as children recognize the need for the adult to act both as a friend to them and as a friend to other adults.

REWARDS AND GIFTS

Because adults have greater access to resources primarily—though not exclusively—pecuniary, the participant observer may feel that it is advantageous to use these resources to develop rapport. This technique can be successful, but it can also lead to difficulties. Researchers may offer many services to child informants, including companionship, educational expertise, praise, food, and monetary loans. A useful rule of thumb when the researcher is trying to be a friend is that one should behave as a good friend might. This involves establishing relations of mutuality and respect that implicitly involve boundaries for acceptable "exchanges."

When in a position of authority, one must avoid misusing responsibility merely to curry favor with the group. Problems may arise, as exemplified in Best's discussion of her research with 6- to 8-year-olds in an elementary school:

> Although I was not a classroom teacher and had no influence over the homework the children were given or the grades they received, they viewed me as a member of the school establishment because I was an adult within the school. I was able to mitigate punishments and facilitate rewards. Thus, when the boys in the third grade formed the exclusively male Tent Club, I was invited to join because, although a woman, I was useful to them. They had guessed, correctly, that I would use any influence I had on their behalf [Best, 1983, p. 2].

Such a stance raises significant questions as to whether children should be protected because of their relationship with an influential researcher, even though this person is not in a position of authority. One wonders whether this manipulation by the children compromises the research. Certainly the researcher in turn manipulates the children for her own ends, but the protection she offers them may undermine justice within the school. It also poses ethical questions about what kind of favors an adult researcher should offer to children in the attempt to promote rapport or to gain access to information.

In his research, the first author did provide services for children. He provided rides for both Little Leaguers and fantasy gamers. He took the preadolescents out for ice cream, to movies, and to baseball games. Excellent data were collected in this way. While the behavior may not have been totally natural, the researcher could ask questions outside of the earshot of other adults whose presence would have inhibited the sharing of certain kinds of information.

In regard to utilizing money, we concur with Whyte (1955) and Wax (1971) that any type of financial arrangement between researcher and subjects has the potential to produce tension in the relationship, but that in some situations financial transactions are necessary to gain rapport. It is imperative, however, that loans not be *expected*. The senior author claimed on occasion that he was out of money when demands for loans were becoming too frequent. At other times, he emphasized that the loan was being given for that time only, and he subsequently had justification for refusing to loan money to that same person.

A danger exists in providing services, even those that are not monetary. Researchers may become accepted for what they can provide, not for what they are. They will be seen as useful only as long as they provide rewards. The relationship may become commodified and instrumental. The senior author experienced this problem in the opening weeks of his first season of Little League research. He carried sticks of chewing gum, careful to chew them in public, and was pleased to provide gum to whomever asked. While this allowed him to become acquainted with the players, it also led to insistent demands for gum. This demand became contrary to his research goals, and after a few days on which the gum was conveniently "forgotten," the requests ceased.

In extreme cases, children may attempt to "blackmail" the researcher into helping them, against his or her best judgment. One of Jules Henry's research assistants reported a dramatic example of this in his study of Rome High School:

> Lila [attempted] to blackmail the Researcher into writing a term paper for her. During the Christmas season when Bill [Lila's brother] took advantage of the mistletoe above the Greene doorway to kiss the [female] Researcher, Lila took a picture of it, and she then threatened to give it to [Bill's girlfriend] if the Researcher refused to write the paper. The Researcher solved this problem by staying away from the Greene house until after the paper was due [Henry, 1963, pp. 208-209].

Such difficulties may not be typical, but, as in the Researcher's example, they may disrupt the research. Some informants are willing to use the researcher for what they can get, just as some researchers use their informants. When researchers are asked to help in criminal activities (see Lowney, 1984; Polsky, 1967), the issues of rapport may become legal and ethical issues as well.

Adult-Role-Related Ethical Issues

Typically when ethical issues are discussed in the literature on ethnography or participant observation, they are discussed in light of relations between peers—actual or theoretical equals. Even when we consider oppressed groups, there is no debate that these individuals should be treated as equals. Yet, let us not pretend that either adults or children would be comfortable if full equality were expected. While it is desirable to lessen the power differential between children and adults, the difference will remain and its elimination may be ethically inadvisable.

If one accepts this perspective, several ethical issues emerge. Researchers must remember that children are "immature" (if only in that their behavior differs from what those in power think of as "adult" or morally proper) and, further, they are not at the age of legal responsibility. A participant observer can justify not interfering with the actions of deviant adults, but such a justification is more problematic when the informants are minors. The ethical implications of participant observation research differs with the age of the children, and we shall discuss the form that ethical issues take with preschoolers, preadolescents, and middle adolescents in the next three chapters. Here we shall focus broadly on three issues that emerge in qualitative research:

(1) the responsibility of the adult in dealing with possibly harmful situations;
(2) the implications of the adult "policing role"; and
(3) the problems of obtaining informed consent from one's informants and explaining the research in a comprehensible fashion.

ADULT RESPONSIBILITY

In dealing with children in unstructured situations or when there is no clear adult authority, one may have to make quick decisions in order to protect the children involved. Children are mischievous, sometimes aggressive, and occasionally cruel. What is the responsibility of the participant observer in that situation? The ethical guidelines of the American Sociological Association (ASA, 1968) claim that the researcher should ensure that research subjects do not suffer harm as the result of their participation, but this refers to circumstances in which the researcher is actively doing something to the subjects. Does it apply to participant observation in which informants are encouraged to behave naturally? Yet, this naturalism is not clear-cut either. Observation is always reactive to some degree. In some situations, an observer's presence may increase the display of aggression among minors (Polsky, 1962; Glassner, 1976)—this gratuitous display of aggression may be a way to "test" the researcher. Can we ever know what are the "real" motivations of our informants?

The judgment as to whether intervention is appropriate should depend at least somewhat on the situation. Children can place themselves in danger. In that event, an adult participant observer has a moral obligation to assist them in a way that is "protective":

> A fight nearly started between Wiley and Bud. At the beginning of the game Wiley had walked along the Rangers' bench knocking off caps from the heads of his teammates. Later, when the Rangers were losing, Bud attempted to get even by knocking off Wiley's baseball cap, and Wiley got angry. I was worried about this because Bud, who was known for his violent temper, was holding an aluminum bat. They pushed each other, but didn't come to blows. I suggested that they should keep their attention on the game and the situation ended [Fine, 1987, p. 229].

Other adults, who might intervene if the researcher were not present, might refrain, believing that the children are under adult supervision. If a possibility of serious physical injury exists, an adult participant observer may need to intervene, even though he or she will thereby alter the behavior of the group.

Few situations are physically dangerous. Boys frequently get into fights, and on occasions girls do as well. In instances of "normal" or "playful" aggression, peer jurisprudence often is able to handle the situation. Many children's groups contain members whose role involves breaking up fights, minimizing the dangers in which others place themselves, and even serving as counselors or amateur medics. High-status boys, secure in their position of peer authority, also have the ability to tell others to "knock it off."

Yet, if a fight had become sufficiently serious, moral concern would have demanded interference. Had a fight caused permanent damage to one or more of the participants, the observer would have rightly been held in part responsible—morally, and, if the observer had a position of authority, legally as well. While this intervention becomes more problematic as the children grow older, the observer has a special role as long as the children are below the age of legal responsibility. The ideal of not influencing natural behavior is just that—an ideal.

There are other circumstances that are not physically dangerous, but reveal behaviors that are generally condemned: racism and theft. On one occasion, the senior author accompanied some Little Leaguers to an ice cream parlor. While there, he noticed to his acute discomfort that the players were stealing candy. A first reaction was that he had the obligation to stop them and insist that they return what they had stolen. This emotion was partly attributable to generalized ethical concerns, the desire to teach these preadolescents what was morally proper, and the personal fear that he might be blamed and publicly embarrassed if these boys had been seen. Yet, he realized that had he made a public display, their behavior would likely not have changed, but he would have excluded himself from witnessing these behaviors again. As a result, the chance to observe this form of preadolescent deviance, rarely examined, would have been lost. In addition, he had by that time become friends with these boys, and reporting them might cause them embarrassment or legal trouble. One tends to protect one's friends in one's research (Johnson, 1975). In fact, the decision to do nothing was based as much on indecision as on moral certainty. It is difficult to make complex moral decisions in the rush of events. Regardless, the decision ultimately was methodologically sound. On the drive home, the boys discussed what had occurred and, by nonevaluative probing, the researcher learned the extent of stealing (or "ripping off") in other circumstances.

The degree of direct involvement in directing the behavior of children may depend on the individual researcher—we all must live up to our personal standards (Polsky, 1962). Gold (1958) has suggested that on occasion it may be necessary to subordinate the self to the role in the interest of research, but, even so, in dealing with children there will be occasions when one's authority should be used to enforce moral imperatives of the self.

ADULT POLICING ROLE

To what extent should adult participant observers allow themselves to police the behavior of their informants on a regular basis. This issue may arise even when the informants are late adolescents. Blanche Geer (1970) reports that she had to make clear to the administration of the college that when she was observing students she would not be a spy or informant for the administration. Nothing is more serious for the participant observer than not to be perceived as an "honest broker." Many groups are concerned about the use of the information that they provide, and the observer rarely gains full access to the private behaviors of the group until they feel that the observer is trustworthy. These first few days and weeks are crucial in determining the success of the research. The "testing" of the researcher is a common phenomenon—an issue that we shall cover with each age group.

Problems of access and trust stem not only from the children's suspicions of participant observers. Adult authority figures may also pose challenges when they attempt to use participant observers for their own ends—not necessarily cynically, of course.[6] Birksted (1976) found that his observation in a school served a useful purpose for the school in that it kept students busy and, in some measure, out of trouble. Yet, he was unable to meet the school's expectations of an adult:

> Since I persisted in spending most of my time with pupils I was only accepted by a few members of the staff. I avoided teaching, and the one class I was pushed into taking ended by complaints about noise from the teacher next door [Birksted, 1976, p. 66].

The senior author felt similar pressures when asked to run practices, umpire, and once to coach a team when its regular coaches had to be out of town. At several times during the research, he was asked for advice about children with minor behavior problems. Although desiring to help, he felt unable to divulge any information. Neither did he feel it appropriate to enforce the rules that the coaches had established. He had made this clear to the Little League coaches before the season and the issue was never explicitly raised; still, he had the impression that other adults would have liked him to take a more active role in disciplining the children. Because of the participant observer's refusal to discipline the children, he or she may be seen as the good guy, while the adult authority is seen as the heavy. The presence of an noncensorious adult in these situations may make salient the fact that the coach is a harsh disciplinarian. Indeed, the members of one team wished that the senior author could become their coach. The presence of an nondisciplining adult can thus complicate the life of the adult authority.

The solution for the researcher embracing the "friend role" is to emphasize to both adults and children that he or she will not be a disciplinarian, and to back that up with consistent behavior. Whenever the observer feels the need to intervene, it should be clear that the intervention is personal, and not because of institutional concerns.

INFORMED CONSENT

When the observer is not in position of authority (and even in certain instances in which he or she has authority), informants must be informed about the nature of the research. We have touched on this issue earlier when considering the participant observer's research role. Here we want to focus more directly on what the informants understand. The need for (and desirability of) informed consent has perhaps not always been sufficiently recognized in participant observation, where secrecy is still common and decisions about permitting the researcher access are seen as the prerogative of adult guardians.[7] In situations where the adult researcher has little authority, it is desirable that he or she provide a credible and meaningful explanation of his or her research intentions.

Even with the best explanation, children will fit the observer's behavior into their own view of the world and will construct that role through gossip (Murphy, 1985). Thus the senior author was asked if he were a reporter, writing a movie like "the Bad News Bears," or with Little League headquarters. In one league, it was even rumored that he was a drug dealer, just as Robert Everhart was accused of being a narc by his high school informants (Everhart, 1983, p. 287). Observers working in school systems are first assumed to be teachers of some kind (Glassner, 1976; Corsaro, 1985; Everhart, 1983). In general, explanations are easier to make to adolescents who may have some vague notions of "research," but can be quite a challenge among younger children.

During the first year the senior author studied Little League players, he was a graduate student, and he explained to them that he was there as part of a school project. This account seemed to satisfy the children. In fact, one preadolescent friend commented that the researcher's teacher had better give him an A "or else!" Children can identify with doing "homework," and explanations of this kind seem to be generally understandable (e.g., Gordon, 1957). Other years, he told the children (and later the adolescent Dungeons & Dragons players) that he was writing a book about them. As is typical in such situations, he was told that he should be sure to include certain events in the book. At times it seemed as if he was treated as the "official" historian of the league.

Perhaps the major theoretical problem that relates to informed consent with children is how to handle confidentiality. Confidentiality is assumed to be necessary in order to hide the identity of specific persons who might be subject to reprisals or embarrassment. The dilemma in the Little League research was that many players preferred, and in some cases insisted, that their real names be used. The possibility of fame outweighed potential embarrassment in their minds. Most players were enthusiastic about being depicted in the book, and some wondered whether they would become famous. Although some of the players were concerned about their parents learning of things they did, most were not. Further, several claimed that they wouldn't mind if others said negative things about them, feeling that they could handle the situation:

> I was talking with Bill Anders and Rod Shockstein about whether to use their real names in the book. Both boys wanted their names used. Rod added that if anyone says anything bad about him, "I will kill him" [Fine, 1987, p. 236].

Despite the senior author's sense that Little League players preferred to have their names used, he decided to use pseudonyms. He considered using the real names of those who requested it, but concluded they were not sufficiently aware of the possible ramifications of their decisions. Several informants made remarks with aggressively sexual or racial content, and, even after several years, they might be blamed for these statements.

While a verbal account is important, actions speak louder than words in informed consent. The actions of the participant observer will be the central way in which children learn of the researcher's intentions. The questions asked, and the situations during which the observer scribbles furiously in his or her notepad, will highlight the observer's true interests.

Informed consent, of course, implies informed rejection. Children must be given a real and legitimate opportunity to say that they do not want to participate in the research. While it is not possible for the researcher to leave the setting simply because of the refusal of one or a few individuals to participate, these individuals should not be questioned, their actions should not be recorded, and they should not be included (even under a pseudonym) in any book or article. To be sure, when these individuals are part of a group, they may be included as part of a collectivity; still, their legitimate rights should be respected. Often these rejections are a result of mistrust of the researcher; at some later time when the researcher has gained rapport with the group, these individuals can be approached again—tactfully and privately—and asked if they have changed their minds. While it is tempting to pressure these individuals, such pressure is unethical. In the senior author's research, he has never had an informant refuse to be observed, and only a few refused to be interviewed.

When one obtains informed consent with children, one will also need to obtain consent and support from adults. This can be more complicated than obtaining consent from children. Indeed, adults often are more concerned about what researchers write than are children (Everhart, 1983, p. 282). To gain access to a league, the senior author first approached the president of the Little League he wished to study. He explained that he wished to examine how Little League baseball players played the game and what they did in their leisure. He described the basic plan of the research—he would observe but would not be actively involved in the league structure as an umpire, coach, or grounds keeper. When he gained the league president's approval, he asked to meet the coaches and other adults involved with the league. This was done at league board meetings or at the baseball tryouts. At that time, he explained the goals of the research—finding out about preadolescent behavior—and told the coaches they could request that he not study their teams—either on specific occasions or for the whole season (this happened only once; described in Fine, 1987, pp. 237-238). He emphasized that he would not undermine their authority. Gaining the approval of the coaches, he asked for permission to explain the research to players. At the end of the talk, each player was handed a letter to give to his parents; it explained the central focus of the research, invited parents to call or speak to him with any questions, and informed them that, if they had objections to their child's participation in the study, their wishes would be respected. Only two parents (neither on teams studied intensively) registered objections, and their children were not interviewed or given questionnaires.

Several coaches admitted after the season that they were hesitant about the research, afraid—in the words of one coach—that Fine "would blow things out of proportion." Coaches (and perhaps parents) were afraid that he would conduct a "hatchet job" on them; eventually they decided that he was "on their side."

On some occasions, attitudes of adults have disrupted research. We mentioned the problems that a leader of a girl scout troop encountered when parents felt that she wasn't disciplining her girls sufficiently. She had to answer to a girl scout council for her behavior. Robert Horan provides an equally dramatic instance in his research with preadolescents:

> I came upon two boys breakdancing on a sheet of cardboard.... I stopped to chat with them.... My two informants ... told me that they'd learned from the breakdancing movies which they'd seen on cable TV.... I mentioned that I had videotapes of [breakdancing] performances. My two informants asked if they could come over to see these tapes; I told them that this wasn't a good time, but perhaps we could do that in the future.... Upon my return [home the next day] my wife informed me that she'd been visited that day by a police detective. He told her that one of my informant's parents had called to complain that their son had been invited to watch movies by a strange man with a large black dog. Naturally perhaps, the fact that I was a folklorist counted for little.... I immediately called the detective. . . . Following my encounter with the detective, I abandoned my plan to investigate the rural white breakdancers [Horan, 1987, pp. 3-4].

Horan's "mistake" was that he started an informal conversation with children (and invited them to his house) before getting to know their parents. We live in a society in which parents are concerned about strangers kidnapping and abusing their children (see Best and Horiuchi, 1985). The ease we had researching children in the late 1970s probably could not be duplicated today. The creation of the "stranger" (or "stranger danger") as a major social concern with parents has posed new and challenging problems for those who wish to understand the world of children. Researchers have the obligation to understand how the concerns of parents affect what can be done with their children, given the images of social problems in society. Likewise, as the legal environment has changed in the United States, researchers may find themselves more responsible for what happens when they are present. The fact that one is conducting research (and being "passive") may still leave one open to the charge of negligence. To the best of our knowledge, such a case has not occurred—yet.

Understanding the World of Childhood

Understanding what children say would, on its surface, appear to be a simple task, but it proves to be deceptively complex. Children have a subculture of their own—a culture of childhood (Speier, 1976; Goode, 1986; Silvers, 1976). Stone and Church suggest that

> children have a special, separate subculture with traditions, games, values, loyalties, and rules of its own. The culture of childhood shares many of the attributes of primitive culture. It is handed down by word of mouth, it includes many rituals and magical formulas whose originals meanings have been lost, it is hidebound and resistant to alien influences and to change [Stone and Church, 1968, p. 370].

This culture, like many grounded in closed communities, has elements that are "secret." It is what Glassner (1976) termed "Kid Society."

Although this situation is somewhat analogous to that of any group that hides its behavior because of possible repercussions, what makes the research challenging is that all adults have passed through childhood, and, as a result, may believe that they have a greater knowledge of children's culture than they actually do. This sense of déjà vu may be deceptive, presenting an obstacle to successful research—in that children's behavior may be interpreted through old frames of reference.[8] For example, the behavioral referents of preadolescent male talk about their "sexual conquests" are different (and somewhat more "advanced") than the behavioral referents of similar talk when we were their age. Because this topic is usually handled obliquely, it may be difficult to discover precisely what behaviors are being referenced. Only after developing trust with the preadolescents could they be questioned. Still, because of the delicacy of the subject matter, and the uncertainty of the children as to what they really meant, the questioning had to be done tactfully.

In addition, because children live within the mainstream of society, there is a tendency to believe that their culture is highly similar to adult culture. While children's culture is similar in some ways, as researchers, we should not take this for granted, and it is wrong to assume that our social meanings are the same as the social meanings of children. Our spatial proximity to children may lead us to believe that we are closer to them than we really are[9]—only differing in that (adults claim) children are still growing up ("developing") and are often wrong ("lack understanding") (see Waksler, 1986). This issue has been effectively made by phenomenologists who have underlined the particular difficulties that adults have in understanding the talk of their children (Silvers, 1983), and who believe that, by successfully overcoming this problem, adults are able to understand much about their own world that is unavailable because of their closeness to it (Silvers, 1976). Much of the unique contribution of participant observation is lost if we ignore or dismiss our informants' social meanings.[10] Likewise, the questions that we adults ask during interviews presuppose an implicit adult theory of childhood or adolescence (Baker, 1983; see also Tammivaara and Enright, 1986).

The situated character of children's meanings is perhaps most evident in the world of insults. Insults are spoken frequently by children with a wider range of meanings than adults might guess: to indicate friendship, status, or disdain. An adult who examines these words on the basis of the expectations of adult society, assuming the standard denotative and connotative meanings that adults give these words (e.g., *fag*, *dip*, or *whore*), may overlook their implications when spoken by children (Fine, 1981). To complicate matters further, one should not assume that these meanings remain constant over generations—or even between curricular cohorts of a single academic year. Meanings can also differ between communities. For example, the senior author noticed that the obscenity "cocksucker" was considered much more hostile when used by preadolescent boys in one community than in another. In one case, it was a fighting word; in the other, it was an amusing obscenity.

Assumptions that might seem valid because we believe that we know and understand children, both because we were children once and because we see them so often, present a methodological problem. Essentially this is a problem of ethnocentrism, but it is compounded because often we do not recognize that it is problematic. Only by attempting to bracket our commonsense understandings and thereby making these neighbors into strangers (and, in turn, making these strangers into peers by taking their roles) can we begin to get a sense of what it means to be a child.

NOTES

1. An exception to this statement are those studies of late adolescence in which observers pretend to be full, hidden members of that culture. In such studies, typically conducted by pop journalists, the observer pretends to be a newly arrived member of a high school class (see Tornabene, 1967; Owen, 1981; Crowe, 1981).

2. For a contrary view of the possibilities of interpersonal closeness, see Damon (1977).

3. Authority lines can be vague at times as in cases of "opportunistic" research in which a researcher has contact with a group of children because of circumstance, rather than a formal authority. Those adults who meet children by virtue of being kin, neighbors, or friends of their parents are not in authority roles, but still have some residual authority by being "adults in the community."

4. Here we do not consider the various types of fabrications that Goffman (1974) addresses. All the world can be an arena for espionage.

5. "Moons are shining" was an expression used by preadolescents in one suburb to describe the childhood custom of "mooning." Mooning has many variants, but essentially it refers to the act of showing one's buttocks in public. In this community, it typically involved a group of boys pulling down their pants and underwear in unison while facing away from a major street. The "moons" shine for no more than a few seconds.

6. This problem is lessened when the researcher is examining youthful "deviant behavior" that is recognized, or even supported, by the relevant adults. In Adler and Adler's (1978) examination of young drug users, their ethical responsibility was lessened because the children used drugs with their parents' approval.

7. The issue of informed consent of children in medical settings is sensitively treated by Langer (1985). She argues that it is important for doctors seriously to consider the wishes of children in planning their medical treatment.

8. Sometimes children may "perform" information gained from one adult in front of another adult from the same background—thus convincing that second adult that children really are knowable and haven't changed that much after all (Peter Adler, personal communication, 1986).

9. A similar argument is made by Peshkin (1984) in studying a fundamentalist Baptist school. Despite the similarity of the school in some ways to secular American society, the differences were dramatic and capable of leading to profound misunderstandings. The children Peshkin studied, although neighbors of "normal" (i.e., secular) children, were very different in beliefs and values.

10. Goode (1986, p. 94), studying a deaf-blind girl, attempted to understand her world by empathizing with her: "Through unique research techniques (mimicking, remaining passively obedient during interaction, prolonged observation, video taping interaction and simulated deaf-blind experiences) I discovered that many of her seemingly pathological behaviors had a definite purposiveness and rationality. The more I 'saw' things from her point of view, the more I realized that because the staff and other professionals had operated with culturally dominant adultcentric conceptions of human competence, they incorrectly faulted these residents."

2. PARTICIPANT OBSERVATION WITH PRESCHOOLERS

It hardly makes sense to think about participant observation with infants. One can observe and interact with them, but can one really "participate" in a meaningful group life? It is not until the child is ready to attend preschool (from age 3 to age 6) that participant observation becomes possible. By age 3, the child begins to belong to a group that is meaningful to him or her, and, as a consequence, group relations can be studied. This period corresponds to that examined by Piaget (1962 [1932]) in which children begin to develop a consciousness of rules (that is, the belief that social relations with other children should be patterned, even if they do not agree on the specifics of this patterning).

The preschool period is a very exciting and compelling age because it represents the initial phases of the child's involvement in a wider social community. Yet, it is an equally frustrating period for study because, by the age of 3, a child may be highly verbal and very active, but it is not always apparent to adults what this talk and activity means. While it becomes tempting to assign one's own meanings to the behaviors of preschoolers, these interpretations are problematic. As an age group, preschoolers have been studied more frequently by psychologists and social anthropologists than by sociologists. Yet, this has started to change with much high-quality sociological research being produced in the past decade (see Mandell, 1984, 1986; Denzin, 1977; Corsaro, 1985).

Those who study adolescents have tended in general to focus on deviance; students of preadolescence, on community and culture; observers of preschoolers tend to be most interested in the development of language and the social relations that flow from language use. This is the period of language acquisition. By the time a child enters first grade, the major portion of his or her language development is complete and what is needed is fine-tuning of these skills. Because this process is cross-cultural, it has been studied by linguists, but not often using the participant observation methodology described here.

In the following two chapters, we will use research by the senior author as an empirical basis for our analysis. Because we have not published on preschoolers,[1] we have chosen to base much of our analysis in this chapter on William A. Corsaro's excellent 1985 monograph, *Friendship and Peer Culture in the Early Years* (see also Corsaro and Streeck, 1986). Corsaro spent a year observing a university nursery school with children ranging in age from approximately 3 to 5 years old. He used a variety of observational techniques, including concealed observation from an observation booth in the nursery school (this school is frequently used for research by faculty at its host university), participant observation, and videotaping. Corsaro's specific concerns in his research were the ways in which preschoolers use language to build a social structure and a culture. Corsaro's research is in our judgment a model for the ways in which researchers should conduct qualitative research with young children—best of all for our purposes, he is explicit about how he went about conducting the research.

We shall also draw heavily on two other sources. First, Andy Sluckin's *Growing Up in the Playground* (1981)—a study of school playgrounds in Oxfordshire in which the researcher does not attempt to establish friendly contact with the children he observes. Second, research by Nancy Mandell (1984, 1986, 1988) in two day-care centers: one in Massachusetts, the other in Hamilton, Ontario. Mandell, in contrast with Sluckin, attempts to develop an egalitarian friendship role with the children she observes.

The Role of the Researcher

Although the goal of participant observation research is to establish equal status contact with one's informants, this is not entirely possible with preschoolers. As we discussed in Chapter 1, the age structure constitutes a major barrier to equal status contact, although some measure of friendship may develop. In fairness, it is important to point out that some disagree. Several researchers downplay the necessity of friendship (although they emphasize "friendly contact"). Thus Coenen conducted research with deaf children without a mastery of sign language, feeling that this would permit a greater focus on "implicit meanings" (Coenen, 1986, pp. 260-261). In a similar way, some anthropologists rely on interpreters to permit them to understand what children are doing (Whiting and Whiting, 1975). Observational and ethnological studies are willing to accept the role-based distinctions between adults and children, even seeing this distinction as a means by which children will not take so much notice of adults (Sluckin, 1981; Blurton-Jones, 1972; Dawe, 1934).

On the other hand, some researchers (e.g., Waksler, 1986) suggest that all components of adult power except physical differences can be bracketed to permit the participant observer to participate in the world of children as a "full member." Waksler (1986, p. 80) argues that "sociologists can suspend their adult role much as they suspend other partisan roles as they carry out research." This position is discussed most explicitly by Mandell, who writes that

> the third membership role, that of an involved participant observer, assumes that adult-child differences are more ideological than previously acknowledged. . . . While acknowledging adult-child differences, the researcher suspends all adult-like characteristics except physical size. By suspending the ontological terms of "child" and "adult" and by participating in children's social world as a child, the central methodological problem rests on essentially a technical question of the extent to which physical superiority prevents adult researchers from participating in the

role of child. . . . I argue that even physical differences can be so minimized when participating with children as to be inconsequential in interaction [Mandell, 1988, p. 435].

Mandell is correct in some regards that the questions are technical, but we feel that they are technical not only in the question of the role of physical size, but they are also technical in the question of how effective phenomenological bracketing can be in such a circumstance. It is easy to claim that one will become a child, it is harder to do it, and harder still to report the experience in such a way that the reader will be convinced that the observer has really gained a *reflexive* sense of what it means to be a young child. It is also uncertain as to how the children will respond to the researcher. Mandell points out that the children that she studied attempted to treat her as an adult and as a teacher. When she refused to play these roles, they were confused.

Our intent is not to dismiss this research style casually; quite the contrary. Mandell and others have thrown down the gauntlet to "more traditional" researchers with children. We hope we will not be seen as unduly cautious if we suggest that various styles of research can coexist and that the evaluation of all styles will depend upon the responses of others to the insight of the conclusions presented. This unique research style is still quite recent and data from these studies are in the process of being published and evaluated. Corsaro (1985, p. 3) takes a more moderate position, recognizing the problems of physical size and social power, but claiming that "the latter problem can be reduced substantially with gradual and, what I term, 'reactive' field entry strategies." While Mandell wishes to be a child as much as possible, Corsaro displays a much more muted, passive role and is placed in an ambiguous status, as in this dialogue with two 4-year-olds:

Betty: You can't play with us!

Bill [Corsaro]: Why?

Betty: Cause you're too big.

Bill: I'll sit down. (Sits down)

Jenny: You're still too big.

Betty: Yeah, you're "Big Bill!"

Bill: Can I just watch?

Jenny: Ok [sic], but don't touch nuthin'!

Betty: You just watch, okay? . . .

(Later Big Bill got to play.) [Corsaro, 1985, p. 1].

This episode nicely demonstrates the peculiarities of Corsaro's role. He does not have the rights of all children; he is seen as something different. His power is still implicit in this episode, precisely because his choice not to use it permits the children to engage in role reversal. He is at their mercy, not a full peer. It is a relation with which he is satisfied. He has a special, undefined relationship with these children: that of a special friend.

Trust

The issue of trust merges with issues surrounding the research role. How can the researcher demonstrate that he or she is a person worthy of respect, friendship, confidence, and trust? One approach is to be satisfied with one's adult role, and to learn what one can while using the differences between adult and child as central to the construction of meaning (Sluckin, 1981). Another approach, that of Mandell (1988), is essentially to "go native," to be a child. A third strategy (Corsaro, 1985) is to let the children accept you, and slowly—reactively—enter their world in the role they prescribe. Let us consider each of these in turn.

Some researchers are unconcerned about developing trust. They are adults, and children around them must be satisfied with that expla-nation. As Sluckin describes his research in playgrounds:

Children are inevitably interested in a strange man talking into a pocket dictaphone and walking round their playground. . . . Those who watch preschool children find that a non-participant role causes them quickly to lose interest in an adult who never initiates any interactions nor responds to any of the children's attempts to make contact. . . . By the end of a month of pilot observation the number of approaches by the five- and six-year-olds had fallen dramatically to practically zero. . . . During the early days I was asked:

Who are you talking to?

What's that radio for?

Why are you following us about?

Why don't you answer? Why don't you answer?

Hey, you Man, speak! . . .

> Within a few weeks the children became more and more familiar with my presence and I became part of the furniture of the playground. On one occasion they used me in a game of "all after that man there" and for fifty seconds I was mobbed, pulled and kicked by a bevy of five-year-olds. Happily, the noise was more alarming than the blows [Sluckin, 1981, pp. 6-7].

The children do learn to trust this researcher, if only in that they find his behavior predictable, and they assume that he will do them no harm, even if mobbed. Yet, Sluckin is quite content to avoid establishing a friendship role. It is important to recognize that he could successfully refuse to provide any explanation for his presence (thereby providing no option for informed consent in this public space). On the other hand, when he observed preadolescents (1981, p. 7), an explanation was demanded in such a way that he could not refuse. This suggests that preadolescents have more rights in controlling their space than do younger children.

The other extreme in the development of trust is reflected in Mandell's least-adult role. As we noted, no one (including adults) was quite sure who she was, so she showed them by acting as much like a child as possible:

> I took to demonstrating to the children, and to the suspiciously watchful teachers, just who I was by swinging on their swings, following them into the sandbox, or hiding with them underneath the porch and in the concrete pipes. At first the children giggled hilariously and the teachers followed me and stared, as if they "knew" that adults didn't do those things unless they were being "silly," out of role. . . . By making myself continually available to the children for interaction . . . and by actually participating in the children's activities in childlike ways, I clearly distinguished myself from marginal or reactive observers. Children's initial responses to being taken as serious and worthy playmates were ones of joy and incredulity [Mandell, 1988, pp. 442-443].

Mandell raises an interesting point. Precisely the same enthusiastic behaviors that make her acceptable to children may make her strange to adults. A new role of regression is introduced whose probable impact is extremely complicated in the social situation. Mandell strives to "make trouble," to complicate the situation, in the name of naturalism (John Van Maanen, personal communication, 1988). As we noted in Chapter 1, the researcher must negotiate acceptance with both adults and children. Sluckin has no problems with the other adults in the situation, whereas Mandell must deal with their suspicions. With regard to trust, it is Mandell's claim that the trust can emerge because children see her as one of them, rather than as an individual engaged in "residual" (or unexplainable) deviance (Scheff, 1966). Of course, a critic might ask how one could possibly know what these children really feel about this strange stranger in their midst—are they as tolerant as Mandell assumes? Preadolescents with their concerns about social differentiations certainly would not be. One also wonders whether an adult *male* could have enacted the role that Mandell attempted.

Corsaro takes what might be described as a middle-of-the-road approach. He is willing to be a friend and a fellow player, but he doesn't push matters. The decision of how his role should be organized is left to the preschoolers. Corsaro describes his methodological approach as "reactive":

> I adopted a simple, what I term "reactive," entry strategy. For the first week in the school, I continually made myself available in peer-dominant areas and waited for the children to react to me. For the first few days, the results were not encouraging.... I observed seven episodes in each session over a 3-day period without any overt response from the children beyond several smiles and a few puzzled stares. [The next day he had been watching some children play.] I then decided to move inside, but as I started to stand up I heard someone say "What 'ya doing?" Sue [a preschooler] had approached me from behind and was now standing next to me in the sandpile. I said, "Just watching." "What for?" she asked, and I answered "Cause I like to." Then she asked my name. I said, and this turned out to be an important reply, "I'm Bill and you're Sue." She took two steps back and demanded, "How did you know my name?"... I now did something I noticed adults do not often do in conversations with young children—I told the truth with no attempt to simplify. "I heard Laura and some other kids call you Sue," I said. [After more questioning] Sue then handed me a shovel. "You wanna dig?" "Sure," I said, and we shovelled sand into buckets [Corsaro, 1985, pp. 28-30].

The process of acceptance proved to be a gradual one. Corsaro was asked a series of questions, was asked to play in various games, and was given a nickname ("Big Bill"), a sign of acceptance. Eventually he was invited to participate in school birthday parties, and received cupcakes and holiday cards. Finally, the children even questioned any authority that he might feel it necessary to use. Given that he was observing within a nursery school, there were many adults available, and exerting authority was not necessary. Still, when he did warn children to be careful, they often reminded him that he was not a teacher and could not tell them what to do (Corsaro, 1985, p. 31). Through his slower integration, Corsaro did gain access to the world of the preschoolers in ways that seemed to make them both feel comfortable, and in ways that the adult authorities did not question.

One of the key indicators of acceptance is when the researcher gains access to the "hidden world" of childhood. Of course, because of the tendentious quality of this material, this access may be difficult. Even by preschool, children know that there are some things that they should hide even from those adults that they really like. They want to permit the participant observer to learn about them, yet they recognize that some things cannot be done to his face. Taping equipment can permit the transmission of information without embarrassment. Corsaro describes the swearing rituals in the nursery school, which always occurred in the peer-dominated areas of the school:

> The two girls, who I will just refer to as A and B, had been playing in the outside yard. We were videotaping their play. . . . I was sitting near the [large wooden] spool holding a microphone. . . . When we found A, she was ducking into a small opening in the back of the spool. She then sat down inside the hollow center of the spool. "Come on in," she said to B. B quickly joined her and, as I appeared in the opening, A said: "Not you! Go away and leave us alone." I said: "Ok, but can I leave my microphone?" B responded: "Ok, but you get out of here!" I was anxious to hear what the girls were talking about, so I motioned for my assistant to let me use one half of the headset and we listened together. The first thing I heard was a banging of the microphone as A picked it up and said: "I'll talk first." She then said "you !!XX, XX, XX!!, !!XX, !X!X,————!" The string of curses was 14 words long and contained some words I had heard only a few times, and two or three I had never uttered in my life. . . . Then they emerged from the spool and I approached and asked them why they were calling me bad names. "You couldn't hear us," said A. I said that I had, and B said: "We weren't talking to you, anyway!" "Yeah," said A, "you didn't hear us anyway." They both turned and walked away, but B looked back and said: "Don't tell teacher!" [Corsaro, 1985, pp. 260-261].

Although Corsaro wonders and doubts whether they realized that he could hear them, one suspects that they knew perfectly well that he could, but simply wanted there to be the *illusion* that he could not. These children wanted to maintain *deniability*. The researcher, in his "insensitive" way, undermines this assumption, making it clear that the claim of

44

secrecy and the line between researcher and child must remain. Perhaps the comments represented some anger at his intrusion on their "secret" space. Note, too, the way in which the researcher treats this "data." Rather than using his usual pseudonyms, these girls get special pseudonyms, "A" and "B." What these girls said is not reported. Although Corsaro assures us that he is not a prude, he apparently is so shocked by this data (and what it implies about these girls) that he cannot bring himself to report it.[2] It has shaken his belief in the "innocence" of these children. Clearly they were savvy in ordering him away; yet, their offering of trust was not fully accepted. Corsaro may have missed some of the natural conflict between adults and children due to his emphasis on obtaining consensus. On occasion, it is hard for adults to accept or handle the trust of children, just as it may be hard for the children to offer it.

Ethical Issues in
Research with Preschoolers

ADULT POLICING ROLE

Traditionally, the adult policing role has not been seen as a concern. Perhaps this is because research with preschoolers is typically conducted in settings where other adults, having formal authority, are present. Consequently, the researcher is not asked to control the preschoolers on a regular basis. Moreover, this research tradition typically requires negotiation of a fairly formal research bargain between the researcher and the adult authorities. As a result, relatively little misunderstanding will occur about the general role of the participant observer. Yet, when a researcher enacts the "least-adult role," there may be some conflict with both children and adults who can't quite believe that the researcher is sincere:

> Crystal is dressed up in black shoes and is carrying a purse. She wanders into the lunchroom, drops her purse and puts on a plastic apron for painting. She starts to paint all over Kyle's painting and on the actual paint board. Kyle turns to me and says, "She's painting my picture." I shrugged and replied "Tell Pam (the teacher) if you want her to stop. I can't stop her. I'm not a teacher" [Mandell, 1988, pp. 451-452].

With older children, this behavior is more explicable, because the rules of preadolescent jurisprudence are suitable to handle the problem, but preschoolers expect adults to settle their disputes, and, no doubt, they had never met an adult who refused to get involved in their world. Children and teachers expect some forms of policing, even if it is only "reactive" policing, that is, responding to a complaint of one child about another.

ADULT RESPONSIBILITY

Although the goal of nonintervention is a legitimate methodological concern, the physical safety of the children being observed must be paramount. Corsaro mentions that, although he wanted to be non-directive, he felt that he had to intervene when an activity might lead to physical injury (Corsaro, 1985, p. 31). Corsaro, with his somewhat ambiguous role, was able to intervene and then to pull back, although he notes that the children would occasionally treat his warnings with some resentment because of his lack of authority.

If one attempts only to observe, one might take that role so seriously that he or she does not intervene, because to interfere would change the natural events that they are witnessing. Those who attempt to note fighting or disputes using a behavioral record methodology (involving formal codes) are most likely to refrain from intervening (see Dawe, 1934, and, for preadolescents, St. J. Neil, 1976).

Paradoxically, those researchers who attempt to enact the child role may find themselves with similar problems, as they may temporarily forget that they are *really* adults. Mandell (1988, p. 450) reports:

Once, on an elaborate pretend fishing trip with four children, I became so immersed in my noninterfering least-adult role that I calmly watched one boy cut open another boy's head with the shovel, ignoring an observing teacher's warnings to intervene and avert the blow. The teacher classified my inattention as negligence.

Her role enactment seems to have been so complete that she was unable to see beyond the confines of that role in order to recognize the consequences that might occur.[3] While this seems to us to be an unfortunate oversight, it may also illustrate the intensity of her equal-status relationship with the children.

INFORMED CONSENT

In some ways, the idea of informed consent with preschoolers would seem like a laughable conceit. How could these youngsters possibly understand the nature of research? Of course, on one level, they cannot. In fact, Corsaro (1985) emphasizes that his research bargain was with the parents (and the teachers), rather than with the children themselves. For instance, the parents had the right to request that their children not be videotaped; there is no implication that the children had similar rights. This is probably reasonable, given the ages of the children. Still, it seems advisable that the children should be afforded some explanation for this strange person at the early stages of the research. Perhaps the children should be told that there will be an adult who will watch and play with them to learn what they like and what they do. This simple explanation might be sufficient to provide a measure of informed consent consistent with the informants' understanding. Our feeling is that children should be told as much as possible, even if some of them cannot understand the full explanation. Their age should not diminish their rights, although their level of understanding must be taken into account in the explanations that are shared with them.

Knowing the Culture

The single greatest challenge for the researcher of the world of preschool is in figuring out what the children mean by the things that they do. By preadolescence, we begin to see the development of meanings that are congruent with adult society, but 4- and 5-year-olds reside in a phenomenologically very different universe. The goal of trying to understand the world of childhood directs researchers to take various stances toward their informants. The assumption, among some observers, is that the closer one can get to enacting the childhood role, the more one will understand what children understand.

There is no doubt that adults tend to understand children from their own adultcentric perspective. Waksler suggests that adults regularly see young children as (1) "unfinished, in process, not anywhere yet" and (2) "routinely wrong, in error, and [as actors who] don't understand" (Waksler, 1986, pp. 73, 76). Similarly, Silvers analyzes Piagetian theorizing as missing much of what it means to be a young child by using adult models of thought. Silvers (1976, p. 49) argues:

> What we attempt to discover about children is dependent on our learning how they comprehend and construct the world, i.e., how their talk or solving of puzzles reveals certain kinds of interpretations and forms of reality, and this is itself dependent on the necessity of crossing over to

share their view of the world. The child's account of what has taken place, or, the reason for something happening, is seen as a possible explanation.

He suggests that we treat the child's explanation as, at best, a partial explanation. He argues that researchers often do not examine the child's world as a legitimate lived reality, although phenomenologists claim that we should (e.g., Denzin, 1977; Waksler, 1986). Of course, the mere assertion that we should explore children's competencies and not their incapacities does not mean that the traditional approaches are wrong. In certain obvious ways, children are "immature" and are being socialized (e.g., Best, 1983; Sluckin, 1981). Both positions present ideological pictures of children, and both deserve to be researched more thoroughly.

Part of the difficulty with achieving a reflexive and interpretive understanding of the world of young children is that children are not able to articulate reflexively (at least in "adult" modes of discourse) the way that their world appears to them when questioned by adults (Cicourel, 1978; Corsaro, 1985, p. 72). Thus the adult may have to do this work by "becoming a child" and using his or her reflexive skills. The assumption is that there will be some similarity between these two visions. Discovering what children "really" know may be *almost* as difficult as learning what our pet kitten really knows; we can't trust or quite understand the sounds they make. We think that we can make sense of what behaviors have just occurred, but can we be sure that we are not reading into their actions? In taking the role of a preschooler or kitten, we may feel we understand their world, but who can tell us that we do? Whatever the prognosis for a feline sociology, the outcomes of a sociology of childhood have been impressive, and while we might still wish to tread softly, some confidence is warranted.

Preschoolers and Observers

The difficulty of conducting research with preschoolers is that often we appear to live in a different world from them. Just as they are struggling to understand us, we struggle to understand them. This form of research is as close as we can come to the traditional anthropological model of ethnography with tribal societies. Douglas Newton's comment (Opie and Opie, 1959, p. 2) that "the world-wide fraternity of children is the greatest of savage tribes" is apropos in emphasizing the sometimes awesome cultural chasm between adult and child.

48

At the same time that we are learning about young children, we must also be guiding them and protecting them. Thus there are special ethical issues that emerge in research with preschoolers that arise in few other places. Only highly protected groups (e.g., the severely handicapped, mentally ill, or developmentally delayed) might be treated in similar ways. Intervention may be an ethical requirement, just as nonintervention typically is in participant observation.

Unlike older children, preschoolers do not have as much say in the research bargain or in the directions of their own action. By this stage, they have learned the rudiments of self-presentation, mostly because of the consequences that occur when they ignore the rules of adults. Yet, their sophistication, according to this adult standard, is imprecise and sometimes naively charming. Thus the adult researcher must take a special responsibility in treating these informants with the respect that all informants deserve.

Whether we find ourselves interested in what children already know (competencies), or whether we are interested in what they are striving to learn (socialization), the issue of change is particularly important for these children. Noticeable changes occur with each passing year, and these are more dramatic than the changes that we see later on. There are many more markers of "accomplishment" in the world of preschool. Even if we take as our task the understanding of the world of preschoolers, it is a continually changing, floating, building world. It needs to be emphasized that the world of a nursery school classroom at the beginning of the year is quite unlike that same classroom at the end of the year, even though it may seem to have been a seamless year. That issue of change has been less studied by participant observers in their research, but it is clearly part of the developmental challenge that qualitative research must face. Most essentially, research of this type is dramatically *developmental* and *longitudinal* in nature. As children change, so do the demands on the researcher.

NOTES

1. The first author spent over two years in charge of a Sunday "day care" at an Episcopal Church, with children aged 2 to 6. Note taking was sporadic, and only one unpublished paper resulted from this experience.

2. We are told: "I should add here that I am not a prude. I have been known to cuss every now and then. Many of these words were references to sexual activity and curses which had to do with the legitimacy of one's parentage" (Corsaro, 1985, p. 261). Perhaps the knowledge of 5-year-old girls should be kept sheltered from impressionable adults!

3. Children themselves at this age can be quite expert at taking care of and comforting each other (e.g., Corsaro, 1985, pp. 177-179).

3. PARTICIPANT OBSERVATION
WITH PREADOLESCENTS

Preadolescents sail the passage between the Scylla of the Oedipus complex and the Charybdis of puberty. In contrast with its stormy neighbors, preadolescence ("the latency period") seems relatively quiet. Although developmental psychologists do not agree precisely on which features distinguish preadolescence from those periods that bracket it, they recognize that the period is more than a way station to puberty, more than a transition between two important stages of development. As Fritz Redl (1966, p. 395) suggested, it is the time when "the nicest children begin to behave in the most awful way." It is a period of "good children and dirty play" (Fine, 1986). Children at this age are testing the boundaries of proper behavior, establishing close friendships, and developing a finely attuned sense of self-presentation. This feature of their activity has implications for research.

The senior author will use his own research study, *With the Boys: Little League Baseball and Preadolescent Culture* (Fine, 1987), as the focus of discussion. Because many references will be made to the senior author's experiences, we have decided to use the pronoun "I" throughout the chapter, rather than the more formal and distant third person. The reader should remember that the research was conducted with suburban white males, and that group will be the basis of analysis. This research was based on three years of participant observation research with ten Little League baseball teams in five communities in New England and Minnesota. The teams examined consisted of 12 to 15 preadolescents, coached by one to three adults. Over the course of a three-month season, teams play 14 to 21 games and, including practice time, spend about ten hours a week together. I observed without having a formal role in the Little League context. My original interest focused on the baseball team itself and its creation of a small group culture, but over time, my focus shifted to observing preadolescents outside of the sports setting, and I came to know these boys as individuals, rather than merely as sportsmen.

The Role of the Researcher

Preadolescents are, as a group, beginning to explore the ways in which they fit into society. They are no longer mere appendages of their families, and, in most instances, they are not closely monitored by their parents or other adult guardians. Unlike the preschoolers described in the previous chapter, preadolescents have the opportunity to develop their own society outside of the prying eyes of adults. They have a rudimentary right of privacy. This means that they have a special right and opportunity to decide the way in which they will relate to the researcher—at least those researchers who do not have formal role-based authority relations over them. They have power to control or contain the research in ways that younger children do not, and the participant observer is at their mercy.

This issue was raised in Chapter 1 when I noted that I was never invited to observe certain kind of pranks and boy-girl interactions. The point here is that the preadolescents had the authority to decide when I could be present, in ways in which preschoolers would never conceive. This power means that preadolescents will have a fair degree of authority to shape the role of the researcher, and the researcher who wishes to gain rapport with informants must recognize this.

It is certainly true that relationships with individual preschoolers may differ—some may like the researcher more than others, and, in turn, the researcher may have his or her preferences. By preadolescence, however, the existence and substantive content of these special relationships become clearer. Not only are there friendships, but there also may be dislikes between researcher and informant. I must confess that I knew some children whom I didn't much like personally, while I found others to be very likable. Some children stayed away from me or were apathetic to my presence; a few were, on occasion, nasty; others became close friends.

This has implications for research. It would not make good sense to speak of the researcher working with preschoolers as having a "key informant"—this role suggests an equality of relationship that is generally unfeasible with children that young, and we know of no study of young children in which the researcher describes a key informant. Such a role can be present by the time one's informants are preadolescents. Indeed, key informants may be more important in researching preadolescents than adolescents, with whom the researcher and informants will share more cultural values and assumptions. In work with preadolescents, the sponsorship of a "key informant" may be crucial to learning the ropes and gaining acceptance by a group of informants. This individual is often cited as the "hero" of research.

In the course of my research, I gained the help of several preadolescents who can properly be termed key informants. In the first league I studied, I received the assistance and sponsorship of a 12-year-old named Rich Janelli, who suggested techniques of gaining rapport with his friends. Without this help, I might have given up in frustration. We struck an informal and unstated research bargain. These children expended their time, energy, and prestige to help me and, in turn, perhaps, gained some status and rewards from their access to me.

Within any population of informants (not merely a population of children), there are several individuals who could potentially take on the role of key informant. One criterion for this role is that the individual has a central position in the social structure of the group, which implies access to persons and knowledge (see also Everhart, 1983). One can distinguish between two components of the key informant role: that of *sponsor* and that of *source*. Needless to say, these two components need not be embodied in the same individual. In the course of the research, many adult coaches and parents acted as sponsors, allowing me to gain access to their charges, but they were unable, despite their best intentions, to provide much information about the nature of children's culture. Some low-status preadolescents provided a wealth of information,[1] but little aid in gaining entry to the group of which they were nominally a part. It is the convergence of ability and willingness to supply the researcher with information *and* entré that is the mark of the key informant.

What kind of child would help in this way? Often it is a child who has a sense of security in his or her position of leadership. These children are self-assured in social situations, and this self-confidence allows them to bridge the gap between adult and child. It also leads them to feel secure in their social authority and competence over a friendly, yet ignorant, adult. The key informants in my research were preadolescent "teachers," willing to suggest ways I should act or react (i.e., don't be shocked; don't be too pushy; don't ignore the middle-status group members). This represents something of an inversion of the normal relations between adult and child. It also represents placing trust in an adult, when normally, because of the topics being considered, that trust would be misplaced.

In my role with these children, they gained from my presence, and this was part of the basis of our relationship. Thus when I did research in Rhode Island, I invited some boys to Boston to a Red Sox game; I took a group of Minnesota youngsters to see *Star Wars*. Because I was not able to invite all children, I took those who had helped me most at that time in the research. Fundamentally, we developed exchange relationships that were balanced, even though different "commodities" were involved (including their desire to be immortalized through my writings and my desire to learn about the world of the preadolescent).

The role that I adopted in my research (and this applies to other researchers as well) was complex. This role certainly fell within the "friend" role discussed in Chapter 1, with elements of such "folk roles" as big brother, student, journalist, and protector. With each boy, however, my role had to be somewhat different. This factor is at the core of participant observation research. The researcher does not have a single, simple, immutable role but is continually shaping his or her role to fit an ongoing relationship. Preadolescents, because they are shaping their own roles in response to peer pressures, can understand this mutable nature of the role being fashioned by the researcher.

Further, because children are fitting their behaviors into standards that they conceive of as characteristic of the adult world, having a "friend" (the researcher) who is also an adult is desirable for their self-image. They can try out certain adult-type behaviors in the presence of this person, while also maintaining their rights to be childish. Much substantive research (Thorne and Luria, 1986; Glassner, 1976; Hughes, 1983; Schofield, 1981; Eder, 1985) has shown the possibilities of high-quality interaction with children and a deep and rich insight into their culture. There are roles available to the adult that permit them to insinuate themselves into the delicate world of childhood.

Trust

As children age, they develop the right to say "no" to the researcher. Typically, of course, they say "yes"—for which participant observers are in their debt. Yet, they want to know how the participant observer will relate to them, what he or she will let them "get away with," and where he or she will draw the line, using the authority inherent in the adult role to control their behavior.

Virtually all researchers who have written on participant observation with children, and particularly with preadolescents, have noticed that the children test the adults. A particularly dramatic example of this was described by Andy Sluckin, who attempted to limit his interaction with the children in an Oxfordshire school playground as much as possible, essentially adopting an observer role. Sluckin describes the reactions of the children:

It is far from easy to stoically ignore a delegation of thirty nine- to thirteen-year-olds demanding, "Can you tell us what you're doing?" I replied, "I'm just having a look round so that I can write a book about playtime." The children were satisfied and left me alone, but on another occasion a group of twelve-year-olds gathered round chanting menacingly, "We've got him surrounded, we've got him surrounded." Since it was impossible to make an excuse and leave, I put on a brave face and joked with them. It turned out that all they wanted to know was, "Hey Mister, can I be in your book?", and how could I refuse [Sluckin, 1981, p. 7].

The point is that preadolescents now have the *standing* to find out what the goal of the participant observation is. They have the right to decide whether to trust this individual, and they may elect not to participate in this research.

The rights of children to control their relations, however, go beyond their right to demand an answer. They also take an active role in testing the researcher by behaving in ways that invite a response. This is particularly true for boys, who are actively encouraged to explore the limits of their sexuality and aggression.

Glassner (1976), who studied children in an elementary school playground, found that they changed topics of discussion when he arrived and that his questions were answered formally, until he had proved that he would not inform teachers or school administrators. His acceptance came only after several incidents in which he observed activities proscribed by the principal (e.g., snowball battles and other fights) and simply wrote down what he observed without notifying other adults. During one incident, several of the children asked Glassner, "What's wrong with you, mister, aren't you going to report us?"

In my own research, preadolescents behaved in similar ways—particularly with regard to rowdiness. This constellation of behaviors included shouting, shoving, fighting, insulting, and arguing. I had to repress my adult desire to intervene at the slightest provocation in order to show that I could behave myself around preadolescent boys.

On one occasion, I was in a park with a group of preadolescent boys who, over a period of about five weeks, had begun to trust me. Suddenly, these boys spotted a group of girls they did not know, seated around a park bench near a thermos of water. One of my companions felt that it would be great sport to bother them (and simultaneously pay attention to them). He and his friends plotted to rush them, steal their thermos, and pour out the contents, disrupting their group. After a short period of insults between boys and girls (mostly about their physical attractiveness), the plan was put into effect—with the expected screaming and squealing on the part of the girls. At one point, several of the girls turned to me (busily taking notes and appearing, I assume, furtively guilty) and asked me, as the adult presumably in charge, why I didn't stop them. This reasonable question placed me in a difficult situation as a participant observer. Because no serious harm seemed to be occurring, and because I felt, from various cues (such as the boys not looking at me) and prior actions, that the behavior was natural and not being done for my benefit, I decided not to intervene, and said only that I was not in charge and had no control over their behavior. The boys were gleeful at hearing this, and shortly, with their mission completed (and the beginning of cross-sex contact begun), left the scene of battle. In retrospect, that occasion seems a significant step in my acceptance as an honorary preadolescent and indicated to the boys that I would not restrain them excessively—that I knew "my place" in relation to the group. After that time, I became more integrated into their group and began to hear more detailed accounts of previously "hidden" activities such as "making out"; one boy even used my recorder to tape a mutual masturbation session, and then returned the tape to me without commenting on what was taped. Clearly I was not a full member of the group, but I *was* accepted as a special member.

During preadolescence, the social worlds of boys and girls are sharply separated (Thorne and Luria, 1986). In the beginning of this period, boys and girls pay little attention to each other. As time passes, there is a start of cross-sex interaction, although it is often clothed in the guise of hostility. Here the sex of the researcher may play a significant role, particularly when the researcher wishes to understand the secret cultures of childhood. Some researchers (e.g., Gregory, 1984) accept the validity of cross-sex ethnography; however, when one's informants are preadolescents, such research is difficult. At younger ages, participant observation poses relatively little difficulty (Best, 1983), but at preadolescence one is pretty well limited to studying one's own sex, unless one is interested in public culture, as in schools (Schofield, 1981) or is willing to be limited to observation (Polgar, 1976). Boundaries of group and community trust are too prominent to be easily overcome.

Although trust is always a variable and is important in every setting, when dealing with preadolescents the issue becomes particularly important because this is a period in which issues of inclusion and exclusion are especially significant for the self-definition of the informants. Preadolescents, perhaps more than any other age group, are concerned about the nature of proper relationships with others—one of the reasons that this period is said to be characterized by close friendship ties (e.g., Sullivan, 1953) or gangs and cliques (Furfey, 1927). As a result, the establishment of trust and its maintenance throughout the period is critical for successful research.

Ethical Issues in Research with Preadolescents

Because preadolescents have increased mobility, increased privacy, and increased knowledge of previously taboo subjects, they pose ethical problems for researchers that were less evident with younger children. Children at this age not only behave in ways that are unknowingly dangerous, but also knowingly and consciously behave in ways that are outside the rules set by adults. They even behave in ways that they know are morally wrong.

How should the researcher respond? Some of these issues were considered in the first chapter, but a few additional points are relevant. Researchers must permit preadolescents to express their own indigenous meanings. Polsky (1967), in his discussion of research with deviant adults, argues that a researcher who seeks acceptance by a criminal group must (1) be willing to break some laws (if only as an accessory to crimes and not reporting information to the authorities), (2) make his or her contacts believe these intentions, and (3) prove that these acts are consistent with relevant beliefs. In the case of preadolescents, the issues are structurally similar. This ethical concern merges with our discussion of trust. Children must be permitted to engage in certain actions and speak certain words that the adult researcher finds distressing. Further, in some instances, the researcher must act in ways that are at least tacitly supportive of these distressing behaviors.

A good example of this problem is racist and sexual talk. In the course of my research—in each of the five leagues I studied—children made racist remarks. One day when I was driving some boys home, we passed some young blacks riding bicycles in that almost entirely white suburb. One boy leaned out the car window and shouted at the "jungle bunnies" to "go back where you came from." The ethical problem was what to do or say in reaction to this (and similar) behaviors. In this instance (and others), I offered no direct criticism, although a few times, when the situation was appropriate, I reminded the boys of the past prejudices against their own ethnic groups—a tactic that seemed particularly effective with Irish American boys, some of whom had not realized that their own group had been the target of bigots. I wanted to avoid being seen as moralistic. I suspect that nothing I could have done would have changed their behavior. The point is that the researcher has to recognize that preadolescents will be exploring the boundaries of proper behavior.

The researcher also has to avoid policing sexually explicit talk. Among the boys I worked with, there was considerable sexual discussion (see Fine, 1981, 1987). Perhaps some of this was designed to test me, as described above, but most of it involved topics and styles of talk that were naturally interesting to these boys. Much of the talk consisted of gossip, for which preadolescents are known (see Goodwin, 1980; Fine, 1977) and that adults find distressing. Again, the ethical issue at this age is what to do about it. Our suggestion is merely to listen matter-of-factly to the discussion, but not to intervene. When we discuss adolescent behaviors, which can trail into criminality, the ethical concerns become different, but most preadolescents are not involved in drug use, grand larceny, and felony assault. The adult responsibility is somewhat lessened when dealing with preadolescents than when dealing with preschoolers, although it is not eliminated entirely.

It should be underlined that, in this discussion, we are focusing on mainstream (i.e., reasonably "well-behaved," nonhandicapped, middle-class) youth; what is suggested about these groups would have to be modified if there were an active drug culture (Adler and Adler, 1978; Lowney, 1984), considerable preadolescent crime (Inciardi, 1984), or if the children had physical, intellectual, or social problems that would require special concerns (Buckholdt and Gubrium, 1979). In researching emotionally disturbed children, Buckholdt and Gubrium felt that they had to "help out" the staff of the institution for emotionally disturbed children on certain occasions, although they tried to avoid this. In fact, this endeared them to the social workers. Even so, the presence of the researcher made social work conferences "more fun" for the children, perhaps because more was tolerated with the researcher present. Ethical rules must be situationally applied with regard to the particular characteristics of the children involved.

Knowing the Culture

Understanding what preadolescents mean and do is somewhat easier than understanding the world of younger children. Yet, there is a penumbra of meaning surrounding the words that preadolescents use. Preadolescence—a period of transition between early childhood and adolescence—is also a period of transition between a meaning system at substantial divergence from that of adults to a meaning system (in adolescence) that is fundamentally similar. The movement between childhood and adolescence proceeds at different rates with different children, and this makes understanding the social world of preadolescence even more complex.

A further problem is that researchers have varying opinions about the degree of difference between the meanings produced and sustained by adults vis-à-vis children. Some researchers suggest that the processes by which preadolescents and adults make sense of their worlds are basically similar:

> I have shown that the playground world is created and maintained by processes that are essentially similar to those by which adults create and sustain their worlds. Some of these similarities are at a general level, in terms of values, attitudes, sex-roles and rituals. Other similarities are at a more specific level; individuals of all ages are skilled at manipulating each other using words alone. . . . The different worlds do not teach lessons that are in conflict, but rather they co-operate to teach the skills, attitudes, values, and beliefs that are appropriate for life at the time and also are a good preparation for later on [Sluckin, 1981, pp. 115-116].

This contrasts with the views of others who have written about this period and have emphasized that sets of meanings and values among preadolescents are distinctively different from those of children. Robert MacKay (1973, p. 31) writes:

> In addition to suggesting that children are competent interpreters in the world, I want to suggest that they are also in possession of their own culture or succession of cultures. . . . If the two claims are correct, that children are competent interpreters of the social world and that they possess a separate culture(s), then the study of adult-child interaction (formerly socialization) becomes the study of cultural assimilation, or, more theoretically important, the study of meaningful social interaction.

Others have emphasized that children have different "interpretive practices" from adults, and that we must understand children on their own terms, not on the terms of the adult observers (Silvers, 1976, p. 48).

We cannot provide any definitive advice to participant observers other than that they be aware of the possible disjunction of the meanings of preadolescents and the meanings of adults. In part this stems from *theoretical* differences about the nature of childhood, perhaps more than over *empirical* disputes. Those who examine preadolescents from a phenomenological point of view often emphasize the distinctive differences in interpretation between adults and children. The arguments on this score have been touched on more fully in Chapter 2, and, as we have pointed out, the younger the child, the more likely will the child have a distinctive worldview that may not be understood through adult logic.

There are no general principles that permit us to specify *in advance* when the assumptions of preadolescent thought and adult conceptions will contrast or overlap. Given that preadolescence is, in part, a time of transition, the issue of meaning overlap will be a particular challenge for the researcher. Tracing the beginning of the adult "worldview" is particularly critical for the researcher interested in processes of socialization.

Preadolescents and Observers

Preadolescence is an intensely social period; a time at which one's social standing with one's same-sex peers has particular importance. This is coupled with a desire on the part of many at this age to test behavioral boundaries and to differentiate oneself from others (Fine, 1986b). These features have implications for the role of the participant observer. The observer can validate the self-perceptions of the preadolescents simply by being their friend. Having an adult who listens to them and who is, to some degree, at their mercy fits into preadolescents' needs for social control. Further, this control over an adult is evident when they attempt to test the boundaries of what is proper behavior under the "sympathetic gaze" of the adult observer. The fact that they can "get away" with behavior is satisfying. We do not mean to suggest that, after the first period of testing, preadolescents are engaging in these behaviors *for the sake of* the observer, but the presence of an adult gives these behaviors a certain piquantness that is probably not as evident at times. Because of the desire of the preadolescent to be validated by those older, it is relatively easy to establish a close friendship with a child of this age, but it must be essentially on the preadolescent's terms. Friendships based on adult standards will not permit the adult to observe the private world of the preadolescent.

This is most evident in the lives of boys, but it also appears true of preadolescent girls as well (Eder, 1985; Llewellyn, 1980)—gender does not limit the existence of deviant or unacceptable behavior, no matter what the stereotype of "boys will be boys" seems to suggest.

The particular challenge for the observer of preadolescence is to tolerate (or at least not intervene in) the behaviors of these children that one finds obnoxious and abhorrent. With their emphasis on social differentiation, preadolescents often make statements that demean groups of which they are not members. In the case of white boys, this means, in particular, racial minorities and girls. Although these behaviors are damaging, as an observer, one is required to make nuanced decisions about how and when to intervene—just as the observer of adult deviants must make difficult choices about tolerating the socially unacceptable behaviors of these groups. Generally speaking, one is an "observer," not a moralist, and it is important to remember that one's research may serve ethical purposes by virtue of revealing information to public attention.

We believe that the richness of the data that can be collected from preadolescents is significant. Most important, this period is a crucible in which the culture, values, and beliefs of adult life are being formed. While there is beginning to be a substantial body of literature on this period, preadolescence remains a "dark continent" that needs to be further explored.

NOTE

1. Whenever one deals with marginal individuals, one must take care in judging the information given. Such marginal children may be so glad to have someone to listen to them that they may say what they think the researcher wishes to hear. As with all data, triangulation of research methods is critical.

4. PARTICIPANT OBSERVATION
WITH ADOLESCENTS

Adolescence has the reputation for personal turbulence, for *Stürm und Drang*. Although we might question how well this evaluation fits the behaviors and worldviews of all who share the period known as "the teenage years," there is no question that many transformations occur in this lengthy time span—a span nearly twice as long as the four-year period usually covered by preadolescence. The themes of sexuality and orientation to the adult world that are initially grappled with by preadolescents become central for adolescents. Successfully dealing with these themes is the mark of the competent adolescent. Being unable to cope is an indication of severe personal trouble. By adolescence, the game of life is being played for keeps, even when the players find the rules somewhat obscure. Adolescents are becoming increasingly similar to adults, even though they are adults with rough edges. This adultlike status and these rough edges have implications for participant observation with those in this age group. Indeed, in adolescence, age begins to decrease in importance as a means of differentiating oneself, and other dimensions of cultural differentiation, such as gender and class, become more crucial.

The data source that we will use in this chapter is the senior author's research with adolescents who played fantasy role-playing games, such as Dungeons & Dragons (Fine, 1983). Fantasy games involve players sitting around a table and acting out (through their talk) various fantasy scenarios—they adopt the personae of knights, clerics, or magicians, and test their skills against monsters, dragons, and other enemies, as played by a referee. The games were played in the evening, so that they didn't interfere with school or after-school work. These players (with a few exceptions) ranged in age from about 13 to their early twenties. We shall focus on the problems of conducting research with those in the middle of the period—from about 14 to 16. We recognize that Dungeons & Dragons, as such, is not directly tied to "adolescent culture," even if most players are adolescents. The players were white, middle-class, and male (older "brothers" of the Little League baseball players). In some ways, the fantasy game players are atypical of adolescents in that they are probably more verbal and imaginative than most, and they may have less direct contact with girls. To bolster this analysis, we shall draw upon research with adolescents that others have conducted.

Before discussing the implications of this research, we want to mention several other bodies of research that have been conducted with adolescents and that comprise distinctly different research traditions. A first tradition is that of British researchers who are primarily concerned with working-class youths—that is, lads. These researchers, more radical than most American researchers, are particularly concerned with the way in which the class system is reproduced. How do adolescents, presumably capable of anything, become resigned to a life of labor. The classic volume of this type is Paul Willis's *Learning to Labor* (Willis, 1981), but it is not unique (see, for example, Hall and Jefferson, 1976; Marsh, Rosser, and Harré, 1978; Mungham and

Pearson, 1976; Ball, 1981; Jenkins, 1983). While the orientations and themes of these books differ, they sharply contrast with most American ethnographies in their recognition of the important role of the labor market, class structure, and political economy in structuring the lives of these "lads" (for a comparable American example, see Everhart, 1983). These ethnographies tend to be much more broadly theoretical than comparable American ones, and it might be more difficult than one would suspect for the informants to recognize themselves in these works.

The second research tradition is the study of youth gangs. The classic study of this tradition, albeit one that did not rely much on participant observation, was Frederick Thrasher's *The Gang* (1927). The other milestone in the participant observation tradition of gang life was William Foote Whyte's *Street Corner Society* (1955), although his participant observation was of young men beyond adolescence. Participant observations of gangs and ganglike groups became a mainstay of this tradition (Short and Strodtbeck, 1965; Yablonsky, 1962; Greeley and Casey, 1963; Liebow, 1967; Chambliss, 1973; Anderson, 1978; Horowitz, 1983). Yet, recently, perhaps because of a decline of gangs or because the gangs that continue have become increasingly violent, this research is not as common. Unlike the British tradition, which tends to differentiate the gang members from the rest of society, the American researchers often make the point that these young gang members are not so different from the rest of us. This point is perhaps most effectively made in Ruth Horowitz's *Honor and the American Dream* (1983), which explicitly illustrates that Chicano gang members share common values with middle-class youth.

As is true for preadolescents, the bulk of qualitative research has been with male teenagers (but see Giallombardo, 1974; Campbell, 1984; Simons, 1980; Horowitz, 1983; Fine, 1986a). Again, it is difficult to generalize to girls on the basis of what has been learned about doing research with boys.

The Role of the Researcher

By the time a child reaches adolescence, he or she is "almost" an adult. Indeed, those who study the history of childhood make the point that the adolescent "role" is a relatively recent phenomenon—perhaps it is even a distinctive role of the modern period in Western societies (Aries, 1962; Kett, 1977; Bakan, 1972). It is surely possible for a child of 15 to be treated as an adult—to marry, have children, hold down a steady job, be convicted of a criminal offense, and the like. Whether this is allowed in any given society is a matter of values, politics, and economics. More vitally, it does emphasize the fact that the researcher and his or her informant could have a thoroughly equal relationship.

In point of fact, this is what most researchers strive for in their studies. For instance, although the senior author had an outsider role when he was observing Little League baseball players, he was a full-fledged member of several groups that played Dungeons & Dragons. He entered the gaming world as a novice, learning from those who were younger, and slowly became more knowledgeable. In time, he became so proficient that, given the turnover of players, he could no longer participate in the group without being the expert to whom everyone turned with questions. While most of those with whom he played were aware of his research, he participated in the game in all ways that they did. While having access to a few resources unavailable to some of them (most notably an automobile and a somewhat wider base of knowledge), in all important respects he was like them. The goal of being treated fully as an equal is more possible in this circumstance.

As we discussed in the first chapter, a truly egalitarian relationship is best exemplified when the researcher actually adopts the persona of an adolescent, and becomes one of the group. The senior author's access to fantasy gaming groups was facilitated because players spanned a wide variety of ages. Being a player in his late twenties was not unusual, although Fine was older than most other players. He could not have passed for a teenager. Some young popular journalists, however, can and do pass for high school students, and so are able to get, they claim, the "inside story." While such a situation ostensibly involves equal relationships, in fact, it involves no such thing. While students project their "primary frameworks," the hidden observer is concocting a "benign fabrication" (Goffman, 1974), thereby preventing the intimate questioning that is the hallmark of most participant observation. There is a tendency, among some, to romanticize this secrecy in the name of avoiding "bias." While such a tactic may promote the collection of certain sorts of information (e.g., deviance), it may prevent the understanding of other forms of behavior because of the inability to ask questions.

Some research with adolescents places an observer in a position of authority. Such an approach carries with it its own threats. While preadolescents test authorities, adolescents sometimes wish to break them, and there may be a need for discipline (see Greeley and Casey, 1963). It is perhaps for this reason that relatively few researchers have studied adolescents from a position of authority; there is too great a division between authorities and adolescents for that lack of equality to produce high-quality research (without miraculously overcoming serious obstacles), in contrast to research with younger children, where such a position of authority does not prevent research.

A related problem that can arise in qualitative research with adolescents results from treating them as "research subjects" rather than people one sincerely wishes to get to know. In Polsky's (1962, p. 112) study of delinquent boys in residential treatment, one of his informants subsequently told him:

> At first when you came in, the guys made an effort to bring you into the group, but you were still a staff member and considered obnoxious. . . . They thought they didn't have any privacy any more because you were around every minute of the day. . . . They felt you were invading the little privacy they did have and disliked you for it. Then you stopped doing that for a while and slowly you were accepted into the group.

Polsky commented that inadvertently he had "rushed" the boys and they felt pressured by it. The problem was less that he was an authority than that he was a researcher, and he comments that at first he did not make enough of an effort to become a friend. As a result, Polsky comments that he had to suffer a considerable period of testing from these boys. The fact that the boys were eventually willing to give Polsky a nickname ("Animal") was a sign that he was accepted, even if not completely (Polsky, 1962, p. 113). The length of Polsky's test reflected the fact that he had not built an equal-status role rapidly enough for these boys to feel at ease with him before he focused on his research problem.

The research role is perhaps more delicate when dealing with adolescents than at any other period of childhood, as sensitivity about one's rights and powers are heightened as full adult responsibility nears. When this is coupled with large status differences (as when dealing with lower-class adolescents or those in total institutions), the research relationship can be very fragile. The researcher must take into consideration the structural barriers already present in society.

Trust

Related to the role of the participant observer is the level of trust that he or she can establish with informants. Because of Polsky's early emphasis on research questions, trust was not immediately forthcoming. In contrast, in the senior author's research with fantasy gamers, he chose not to introduce himself as a researcher the first few times he interacted with them. In part this was a function of the fact that he was not sure immediately that he wanted to study the group (see Fine, 1983) and in part it was due to the fact that he had to spend the first few group meetings simply learning the rudiments of this strange and complex leisure activity. Eventually he did explain that he was a sociologist, but by then he had already become a known entity—a friendly acquaintance.

In light of the development of trust, the senior author's research with Dungeons & Dragons' players was relatively unproblematic. When adolescents are acting out in aggressive or sexual ways, however, trust becomes more difficult to establish and relationships can sometimes blow up in the researcher's face. Frank Coffield (Coffield and Borrill, 1983), for example, attempted to conduct participant observation at a government-supported "club" for unemployed adolescents in a housing estate of an industrial city in northeast England. As Coffield tells the story, he may have "rushed" these boys and hence ignored warning signs. He faced a structure that was well recognized by all longtime participants. By the fourth week of research, he had only begun to establish some trust. By choosing to intervene in a situation where the adult authorities had not enforced the rules systematically, he left himself open for attack. Although the key incident is highly atypical, it is worth quoting at some length because it demonstrates the depths to which relations in a research situation can sink. Prior to this critical incident, the young people (varying in age from 10 to their twenties) had smashed the glass door, urinated from the roof, thrown darts at each other, drank beer, sniffed glue, drawn obscene graffiti on the walls, destroyed one of the inside walls, and unzipped the trousers of a worker. Earlier that evening, the observer had to separate two girls who were fighting, only to be accused of hitting them and touching their breasts. The situation was clearly one of incipient anarchy:

> Two boys had . . . forced open a cupboard. . . . They found squares of thick cardboard which they began flicking across the room and into the faces of the children. One girl of 8 received a slight cut just below her eye and so I decided to point out the dangers to the boy responsible. He immediately challenged me to a fight outside and began pushing me in the chest. I explained to him that the cardboard was thick enough to give someone a

serious eye injury and turned away. Ricky, a 12-year-old, straightaway flicked a card into my face. The immediate group became quiet as they waited for my response. I told him quietly but firmly that, if he did that again, he would have to leave. He smiled, picked up another card, and flicked it into my face. I told him he would have to leave, took him by the arm, and began moving him toward the door. After only a few steps he broke from my grasp and began flaying around in all directions with his arms and feet; he then started throwing chairs and knocking over tables. His face was red, his lips were flecked with spittle and his words became incoherent. [His brother calmed him down.] . . . Because of the confrontation I was now accused by one boy after another of "picking on Ricky," and challenged to fight outside. . . . When the club closed, I went outside and was immediately surrounded by the older boys who began pushing and jostling me and telling me that I was about to be beaten up. The other workers, who were returning the equipment to the caretaker's house, ran across and formed an escort round me. . . . We were threatened with stones, half-bricks and the odd bottle; some of these objects were thrown but none landed on target. As the boys closed in on us from each direction, we began to be punched and kicked. . . . I plunged through the boys who had blocked off the pavement by positioning themselves between the railings and the wall of the bridge, and, pursued by the whole group and a shower of missiles, I reached the main road where [a bus had stopped]. . . . Some female passengers began shouting hysterically, as the front runners, Tom and Andy, now tried to board the bus. They both shouted obscenities and spat in my face, as I pushed them off the bus; at the same time I avoided the half-brick with which Tom kept trying to hit me on the head. Eventually, the driver drew away from the kerb, as the whole group of boys arrived and began kicking and hammering on the sides of the bus [Coffield and Borrill, 1983, pp. 533-534].

If nothing else, this incident suggests the effects that a participant observer can have on a situation, and the dilemmas he or she must face. More important, it emphasizes the importance of establishing a set of rules that are agreed to by all parties and subsequently followed. Fortunately, most of us do not have to confront situations that are similar to this debacle, but minor outbursts do occur. Unlike the world of preadolescence where behavior is rarely dangerous, the angry or disruptive adolescent can pose a significant threat to others, a point we shall develop when considering ethical issues. Here we point to the potential consequences of the absence of trust and the lack of clearly agreed upon rules.

The chaotic situation developed as a result of the participant observer attempting to discipline an especially volatile boy. In retrospect, it is clear that one should not make a threat that one doesn't plan to carry out. Just as the boys were testing the observer, the observer tested Ricky. Although the researcher didn't realize it at the time, Ricky had a special role in the group. Ricky had a history of "explosive behaviour," and his friends were tolerant and understanding of him (Coffield and Borrill, 1983, p. 538). Coffield unintentionally broke the norms of the group by his intervention, in a way that would not have occurred had he challenged a boy with more impulse control. The developing relationships were irreparably broken by this incident and the research was terminated.

Coffield honestly addresses his own "culpability" in the matter:

> I arrived at the club a few minutes late because of protracted meetings over reductions in the staff of the department in which I work and was consequently anxious and tired. As the "aggro" developed, my own masculinity and that of the other workers became involved. As is painfully obvious with hindsight, the action I took was in no way planned: I reacted immediately and thoughtlessly [Coffield and Borrill, 1983, p. 539].

Coffield's honest account recognizes that at least some part of the trouble may have been his fault; he helped turn the situation into a "character contest." Further, he recognizes that many of the actions of a participant observer are "natural" in the sense of not being explicitly planned to achieve an end and are not entirely thought through. Finally, he underscores his own humanity. All of us have some level of aggression, touched off by frustration. And he was frustrated that day. Perhaps on some level he enjoyed asserting his authority.

Further, by adolescence, the characteristics of the researcher do make a difference. The fact that Coffield represented a different class in a highly class-marked society probably provoked resentment. Indeed, all those who study adolescents in the underclass must recognize that they are different in a critical respect from those they study—and that their informants realize this. The race and sex of the researcher are critical. Who the researcher is (in terms of societal categories) tells the informants a lot about this person's attitudes and whether he or she is likely to be a good bet as a friend or confidante. In fact, it would be difficult for a man successfully to observe a group of girls (at least outside of a formal situation, such as school). Women have a somewhat easier time in that the boys can cast them in a special, nonthreatening role (e.g., a big sister; Horowitz, 1983, p. 10)—but even here care needs to be taken.

Ethical Issues in
Research with Adolescents

CRIMINAL ACTIVITY

As we have emphasized, the behavior of adolescents can be consequential for society. Teens do commit crimes. In fact, strictly speaking, many of the behaviors leading up to the incident Coffield described were illegal, and Coffield (and the other workers) did nothing about them. In the senior author's research, at several games players passed around marijuana joints, and he politely inhaled on the community toke. Howard Polsky, twenty years earlier, had a similar experience, although in that case the situation was explicitly a test of the observer to see if he was "a good guy" and the cigarette was filled with tobacco (Polsky, 1962, p. 110). When he showed that he would not be forced to do anything (one of the boys had pulled out a switchblade), but that he was willing to go along with the ritual, he was accepted. Various acts imply differing amounts of criminality, and decisions are inevitably made in specific situations, rather than in general.

Outside of the vague assertion of Greeley and Casey (1963) that they presided over the termination of a gang, researchers have typically gone along with the group that they were studying. This is perhaps most extremely exemplified in the vague but chilling references of James Patrick, who studied a violent Glasgow gang. In conducting this research, he posed as a member of the gang, and was known only to the gang leader. Patrick (1973, p. 53) mysteriously describes his involvement:

> I had to take part in the action—in some role or other—and be seen to do so. How and to what extent I was able to comply with this requirement I am advised not to disclose. But I feel I must make it clear that at no time did I carry, still less use, a weapon.

Patrick describes himself as being in trouble for not fully participating in the gang's fights, but there is no evidence that he attempted to stop them nor did he report these gang members to the police, even though their activities were extremely violent. He made certain ethical choices that he had to live with, and that affected his research report. Likewise, Lowney, a self-described "nonparticipant" observer studying a group of drug users, served for these boys as a "father figure and an interventionist." Lowney claims (1984, p. 433) that

> the role of nonparticipant observer *of* deviancy tended to preclude the dilemmas raised by moral, legal, and ethical questions that participant-observers *in* deviance must sometimes face. The nonparticipant role further protected the researcher from compromising his personal values, and made functioning as an interventionist more credible.

While Lowney's position probably represents the general received wisdom in qualitative research, the problem is not quite so simple. By his presence and tolerance, Lowney is supporting chemical dependency, a problem that is recognized as more serious now than it was in the early 1970s when the research was conducted. These adolescents are legal minors, and one must wonder whether the researcher who "enables" drug dependency or who permits crimes to occur is really acting in accord with the presumption of "doing no harm." Although most researchers might opt for not interfering with these crimes or not reporting them, the issue should be squarely and honestly faced by all who choose to work with adolescents of whatever social position or character.

SEXUAL BEHAVIOR

Although adults may not like to admit it, sexuality is often a central concern for adolescents and preadolescents. As such, it naturally becomes a salient issue in participant observation studies of these age groups. When we (as researchers) gain access to the daily worlds of adolescents and preadolescents, we become more privy to some of their secrets, experiences, and interactions that have sexual overtones. In turn, in order to provide an honest and accurate portrayal of the intricacies of their life-worlds, we are required to engage in data collection and analyses that address sexual issues.

Yet, both the gathering and the handling of related materials may present challenging questions to field researchers. For instance, researchers may experience feelings of discomfort when overhearing "dirty talk" or discussions of sexual feelings and activity. On the one hand, a researcher may need to grapple with his or her inclinations as an adult to censor or express disapproval of sexual talk or interaction on the part of minors. On the other hand, he or she may feel uneasy (or "voyeuristic") about being a party to such disclosures because of the norms of privacy and propriety that surround sexual matters. Most important, the researcher will have to make decisions about how to resolve these feelings in order to avoid being unduly reactive in the research setting. We suggest that a researcher can adopt a nonjudgmental approach that does not suppress the sharing of sexual information but that also avoids responding in either tacit or overt ways that make sexuality issues more salient than normal for those being studied.

In general, researchers need to remember that collection of data pertinent to sexuality issues is potentially controversial. They also need to be wary of how it might be used to compromise their research. We had earlier cited an example in which a photograph was taken of a teenage boy kissing a female researcher and subsequent attempts were made to "blackmail" her into providing assistance with schoolwork. Although this did not pose a serious problem, it suggests the ways in which sexually related materials or information might be manipulated in an effort to compromise a researcher.

We also alluded previously to the heightened concerns that parents currently have about adults who are relating to their children. In light of these concerns, the researcher could be placed in difficult circumstances if informants chose to report selectively some of the conversations or exchanges occurring while he or she was present. The parents, of course, would probably become quite upset and concerned if they found out that their children had been discussing issues of sexuality with (or around) an adult they did not know well.

The sexuality issue may also arise in another dimension of research relationships. So far as we know, one issue that has not been broached in the literature of adolescent studies has been the possibility of serious sexual attraction between adolescent informants and adult researchers. Given the fact that both adolescents and researchers are sexual beings, we suspect that such feelings have arisen on occasion. Horowitz (1986, pp. 420-421) indicates that the Chicano gang members eventually flirted with her, but she emphasizes that such flirtation came to nothing. No one has yet, however, openly discussed or acknowledged encountering a scenario that led to intimacy in their studies nor has anyone grappled with the implications or problems it poses for the ongoing conduct of research.

While it is not in the scope of this book to discuss this issue, we believe that it merits more honest and substantive discussion among those who do observation studies with minors (or with adults). We suggest that this kind of dialogue might best begin with a more open sharing of related concerns or situations. In addition to this, researchers might give more serious consideration to developing methods or mechanisms that could be helpful in safeguarding both minors and researchers from sexual entanglements. While it would be easy simply to condemn such activity or to pretend it does not exist, this does not seem to be a very responsible way of addressing this issue.

Knowing the Culture

The hermeneutic problems inherent in research with adolescents tend to be somewhat less daunting than those salient in research with younger children. Perhaps the major obstacles to understanding the world of adolescence derive, not from age, but from class, ethnicity, and culture. One of the challenges for Margaret Mead (1928) in her classic study of the sexual patterns of adolescents in Samoa was to understand what sexuality and adulthood meant from their perspective. The difficulty of this task left her open to criticism from other anthropologists who suggested that she had misunderstood the world in which her informants lived (Freeman, 1983). Mead came to Samoa with questions developed through her experiences with American adolescents and, of course, found significant differences. One wonders whether the American model was even relevant as a model by which to differentiate these Samoan adolescents, who surely were not reacting "against" that paradigm. Mead also arrived in Samoa with her own vision of what American adolescence was like, and it is important to recognize that, even though she was "close" to this scene, her view was no more "objective" than her Samoan data could ever be. As researchers, we may actually be more careful about our assumptions of "exotic" cultures than with our assumptions of those cultures of which we are a part.

One senses similar problems when middle-class researchers attempt to understand lower-class children. They violate the rules of middle-class society, but how do we discern the world from their point of view? And, how do we understand the middle-class culture from which we critique lower-class culture?

As we suggested earlier, middle-class adolescents have been studied relatively less than their lower-class counterparts, and various explanations have been put forward for their behaviors—often in their own words. Words, of course, are not the same as meanings, and one might wonder to what degree these adolescents (or any of us) are able consciously to conceptualize their worlds. As Carolyn Baker (1982) suggests in her article "The Adolescent as Theorist," theoretical activity is a practical and occasioned event—in other words, it is not a given, but is situationally contingent. One cannot speak of an "adolescent (or adult) theory" that one carries around in one's head. Rather, a "theory" in this context refers to a set of viewpoints from which one can construct speeches in addressing a particular situation.

Adolescents and Observers

We have described those features of research with adolescents that in our view differentiate it from research with younger children. The actions of adolescents, more than is true for younger children, are consequential to the community. Adolescents have the opportunity to make important decisions for themselves, and may do each other grievous harm. Adolescents are in a position in which they have the skills to do virtually all those things that adults do, but they don't have the social right to do them or they don't have the judgment (according to adults) to make the right choices.

This raises the ethical choices that we have discussed above. Should the observer be placed in a position of *in loco parentis*? Do researchers have a responsibility to protect adolescents from themselves? In the case of younger children, the answer is surely in the affirmative, and with adults, the answer is commonly negative. Even outside of the rule of law, does the researcher have the responsibility to be a moral exemplar or teacher? The fact that these children are "nearly adults" makes this role problematic.

The issue of trust is also affected by this position. Adolescents can and do regularly make decisions about their own lives, and this implies that they can test the researcher to see if he or she accepts their values and will act upon these values. The participant observer does *not* have the right to do whatever he or she wishes with adolescents, rather, they have the right to direct him or her—within certain social parameters. The dramas of this period make the challenges that the observer faces real and occasionally dramatic. To observe adolescents means giving up some of one's ascribed, age-based "authority" to learn about a world physically close and cognitively similar, but often emotionally and socially distant.

5. TO KNOW KNOWING CHILDREN

The title of this book is a sly entendre. "Knowing children" is both a goal of participant observation with minors and a description of the "lived experience" of these youngsters. We have underlined in this book our beliefs that (1) participant observation with children can be a practical method of collecting valuable data from children, and (2) that participant observation with children depends on different assumptions than participant observation with adults.

Learning from Children

Although it was not our objective to discuss the research findings that have resulted from qualitative research with children, in this summary some of the range of these findings deserve mention. Basically, research with children can be grouped into three categories: studies that find that children are more mature or capable than expected, studies that find that they are more tendentious or rebellious, and studies that find that children change (are socialized) in ways directed largely by themselves.

MATURITY

Some studies find that children are much more sophisticated than we have given them credit for being. They are more verbally effective, emotionally considerate, or socially knowledgeable. They are more "mature" than we as "grownups" believe. We know of no study that has found that children are more "childish" than we have given them credit for. In part, perhaps this is a function of popular ideologies of childhood that emphasize children's lack of knowledge (e.g., Waksler, 1986), but it may also be a function of social scientific ideologies that want to make the work more important by making their informants appear more talented.

The research by Pulitzer Prize winner, psychiatrist Robert Coles (1967, 1986, see also Cottle, 1972), nicely demonstrates how young children in difficult circumstances can keep their heads while all around them are losing theirs. Who can ever forget the good sense and quiet wisdom of Ruby, the young black child who attends an all-white school in New Orleans in the early 1960s, despite the protests of white parents? The "children of crisis" are fearful, but they are also courageous. In Coles's somewhat romantic vision, they are the way that adults *should* be. Other studies, with other theoretical or political perspectives, likewise testify to the skills or competencies of children. Corsaro (1979) finds that children are remarkably skilled at ordering their social lives in quite complex ways, determining who should be able to enter a group. Denzin similarly points to the remarkable sophistication of the play of very young children with each other. In Denzin's (1977, p. 166) view:

> They learn to attach different meanings and interpretations to self, other, and object; and to take the point of view of civil-legal, polite-ceremonial, and relationally specific rules. They learn how to form, break, and challenge social relationships; how to measure time and its passage; and how to assume (or avoid) the biographical consequences of any set of actions. The player at play is seen as acquiring the skills requisite for future moments of focused interaction.

Suffice it to note that these are merely representative studies that demonstrate that children have considerable emotional, social, and cognitive capacities for which we do not always give them credit.

TENDENTIOUSNESS AND REBELLION

A second body of studies remind us that childhood and adolescence need not be a socially placid time. In some ways, these studies connect to the studies that emphasize the "maturity" of children. Yet, these studies highlight the underside of social life. Young children know a lot that we wish that they didn't know (Fine, 1986). Studies of preadolescents find that sexual talk is common and explicit in the "latency" period (Fine, 1981; McCosh, 1976; Knapp and Knapp, 1976; Turner, 1972). Likewise, studies by Martinson (1981) find that children's sexual activity is more extensive than we might like to believe. Analyses of drug use (Adler and Adler, 1978) and prostitution (Inciardi, 1984) point to considerable sophistication at an earlier age than is commonly thought. Those who examine the underside of children's society—their secret education—discover a wealth of nasty, aggressive pranks and tricks. Brian Sutton-Smith, one of the scholars who first attempted to demystify and deromanticize childhood, has demonstrated through historical materials that children are often cruel to each other (Sutton-Smith, 1981; see also

Chandos, 1984). Recent ethnographic studies reveal the same aggressive behavior (Fine, 1987; Virtanen, 1978; Harris, 1978; Jorgenson, 1984; Mechling, 1984) that the historical studies demonstrate.

Adolescents often display their rebelliousness and hostility toward adult authority. One might imagine that these studies of adolescents, perhaps to a greater extent than those that focus on younger children, are grounded in a particular social history and locale. There is no reason to believe that alienation is a constant in the lives of adolescents; rather, it is dependent on the immediate circumstances and structures in which adolescent activity is embedded. The brilliant study by Paul Willis (1981) of the social reproduction of social class position exemplified the British stratification system in the 1970s. No doubt, the issues raised apply beyond his ethnographic time and place, but how far they apply is an empirical question. Everhart's (1983) examination of an American high school suggests that some of the themes of alienation, working-class culture, and resistance apply, at least in an attenuated form, to certain American schools.

SOCIALIZATION BY PEERS

It is perhaps unremarkable that researchers should be interested in the way that children change. Their changes surely appear to be greater and more insistent than the changes of adults. The existence of numerous stage theories gives testimony to the importance given to the changes of children; the comparative shortage of stage theories of adult life suggests that change is not seen as crucial over the age of consent. Change can be "motivated" from many sources: biology, adults, and peers. All three have been studied at length. Ethnographic and qualitative studies of children, however, have focused on how children socialize each other. This theme is evident in the studies both of maturity and of tendentious behavior.

The studies that focus on maturity often examine how children teach each other subtle, often linguistic, skills that permit them to succeed in adult-oriented worlds. Maynard's (1985) or Goodwin's (1982) examination of argumentation among children demonstrates that these are skilled rhetors, and that these skills are being *taught* through the process of discourse. Likewise, children teach each other the rules of gossip— and moral evaluation in general—through doing it (Fine, 1977, 1986a). Examinations of tendentious behavior also suggest a process of peer socialization. The secret education of childhood is part of socialization.

Such talk enables children to enact social roles that will be expected of them as they age. Boys who learn about sexual topics from each other are practicing enacting a male role (Fine, 1976, 1987; Thorne and Luria, 1986), and eventually for getting by as adolescents and adults. Because participant observation has focused on studying groups, it is only natural that the emphasis will be on groups of children—that is, on peer groups and on equal-status socialization.[1]

Different Assumptions About Participant Observation

The primary justification for this book is the fact that participant observation with children poses different problems than research with adult subjects. We suggest that these dissimilarities can be emphasized by the "three Rs" of participant observation with children: responsibility, respect, and reflection.

RESPONSIBILITY

We do not believe that the adult participant observer can ethically take the same laissez-faire attitude with underage informants that he or she might adopt with adults. Children may need to be protected from the consequences of their actions. This is particularly true because the very presence of an adult conveys certain messages to other adults in the vicinity: that the children are being watched over. Adults feel a moral responsibility for all children. This moral responsibility is important, and should not be casually dispensed with. We have emphasized that participant observers should be careful about being placed in a position in which they are responsible for policing the behavior of children and, as a consequence, see their positive relations become truncated. Still, intentionally standing by while a child injures him- or herself or others is surely the devil's bargain.

RESPECT

The core of successful and effective participant observation with children is *respect*. While this is central to all participant observation, with children, it is an additional challenge, possibly because adults often do not show respect to children. Respect thus must be a specific methodological technique, overthrowing the "natural" adult tendencies both to take children for granted and to accord them a provisional status, depending on how their behaviors accord with adult standards. The belief that children are inherently "wrong" when they disagree with adults is an obstacle to be overcome. Further, and perhaps more problematic for participant observation, is the recognition that children have the right to say "no" to research. The essential tenet of informed consent is that the informant has the option as to whether he or she chooses to participate in the research. Even though rejection from someone of "lower status" may be hard to accept, such rejection must be accepted. Children have opinions and make judgments, and even if these judgments are not always those that would be made by an adult, they have the same moral legitimacy.

REFLECTION

Because all adults have passed through childhood, they should *in theory* have some competence in understanding how children feel. Those of us who are parents recognize that this is no simple task. We casually forget much of what we felt and knew. Yet, our own experiences, if properly mined, can be a valuable resource for research. While we doubt the general validity of becoming a child through behavior, there is validity in attempting to role-play the meaning of childhood. The phenomenological validity of attempting to understand the life of a child on his or her own terms is essential. Further, it is an approach that differentiates this type of participant observation from most others in which we have never experienced the emotions, social position, or even some of the culture of the group being studied. The fact that we have all been children gives this research a patina of mundane life that must be overcome, but it also provides a basis of access for those who are able to breech their own well-constructed defenses.

A World of Their Making

Like many written works, this, too, can stand as a bully pulpit. But, aside from all of the intellectual justifications and sage advice that we have presented, we must confess that getting to know children is fun. Having a role that downplays one's authority removes many of the hassles of parenting. One experiences the joys of parenting without incurring the costs. What better way in which to spend a second childhood than to spend it with those similar to those with whom one spent the first. While children are constructing their own worlds, they sometimes permit us to stand with them to enjoy the monuments that they have made.

NOTE

1. The exception to this is studies of collective socialization, such as sport teams (Fine and Kleinman, 1979; Yablonsky and Brower, 1979; Vaz, 1982) or classrooms (Bossert, 1979; MacKay, 1973). Because these are groups as well as settings, traditional ethnographic techniques may be used.

REFERENCES

Adler, P. and P. Adler. 1978. "Tinydopers: A Case Study of Deviant Socialization." *Symbolic Interaction* 1:90-105.
———. 1984. "The Carpool: A Socializing Adjunct to the Educational Experience." *Sociology of Education* 57:200-210.
———. 1986. *Sociological Studies of Child Development*. Vol. 1. Greenwich, CT: JAI Press.
———. 1987. *Sociological Studies of Child Development*. Vol. 2. Greenwich, CT: JAI Press.
Ambert, A. 1986. "Sociology of Sociology: The Place of Children in North American Sociology." In *Sociological Studies of Child Development*. Vol. 1, edited by P. Adler and P. Adler. Greenwich, CT: JAI Press.
Anderson, E. 1978. *A Place on the Corner*. Chicago: University of Chicago Press.
Aries, P. 1962. *Centuries of Childhood*. New York: Knopf.
ASA. 1968. "Toward a Code of Ethics for Sociologists." *American Sociologist* 3:316-318.
Bakan, David. 1972. "Adolescence in America: From Idea to Social Fact." Pp. 73-89 in *Twelve to Sixteen: Early Adolescence*, edited by J. Kagan and R. Coles. New York: Norton.
Baker, C. D. 1982. "The Adolescent as Theorist." *Journal of Youth and Adolescence* 11:167-181.
———. 1983. "A 'Second Look' at Interviews with Adolescents." *Journal of Youth and Adolescence* 12:501-519.
Ball, S. 1981. *Beachside Comprehensive*. Cambridge: Cambridge University Press.
Best, J. and G. T. Horiuchi. 1985. "The Razor Blade in the Apple: The Social Construction of Urban Legends." *Social Problems* 32:488-499.
Best, R. 1983. *We've All Got Scars*. Bloomington: Indiana University Press.
Bierman, K. L. and L. Schwartz. 1986. "Clinical Child Interviews: Approaches and Developmental Considerations." *Child and Adolescent Psychotherapy* 3:267-278.
Birksted, I. K. 1976. "School Performance Viewed from the Boys." *Sociological Review* 24:63-78.
Bossert, S. 1979. *Tasks and Social Relationships in the Classroom*. New York: Cambridge University Press.
Blurton-Jones, N. 1972. *Ethological Studies of Child Behavior*. New York: Cambridge University Press.
Buckholdt, D. and J. Gubrium. 1979. *Caretakers*. Beverly Hills, CA: Sage.
Campbell, A. 1984. *The Girls in the Gang*. New York: Basil Blackwell.
Chambliss, W. J. 1973. "The Saints and the Roughnecks." *Society* 11:24-31.
Chandos, J. 1984. *Boys Together*. New Haven, CT: Yale University Press.
Cicourel, A. 1978. "Interpretation and Summarization: Issues in the Child's Acquisition of Social Structure." In *The Development of Social Understanding*, edited by J. Glick and A. Clarke-Stewart. New York: Gardner.

79

Coenen, Herman. 1986. "A Silent World of Movements: Interactional Processes Among Deaf Children." Pp. 253-287 in *Children's Worlds and Children's Language*, edited by Jenny Cook-Gumperz, William A. Corsaro, and Jurgen Streeck. Berlin: Mouton de Gruyter.

Coffield, F. and C. Borrill. 1983. "Entree and Exit." *Sociological Review* 31:520-545.

Coles, R. 1967. *Children of Crisis*. Boston: Little, Brown.

———. 1986. *The Moral Life of Children*. Boston: Houghton Mifflin.

Conger, J. J. 1971. "A World They Never Knew: The Family and Social Change." In *Twelve to Sixteen: Early Adolescence*, edited by J. Kagan and R. Coles. New York: Norton.

Cook, L. A. 1945. "An Experimental Sociographic Study of a Stratified 10th Grade Class." *American Sociological Review* 10:250-261.

Corsaro, W. A. 1979. "We're Friends, Right?: Children's Use of Access Rituals in a Nursery School." *Language in Society* 8:315-336.

———. 1985. *Friendship and Peer Culture in the Early Years*. Norwood, NJ: Ablex.

———. 1986. "Routines in Peer Culture." In *Children's Worlds and Children's Language*, edited by J. Cook-Gumperz, W. Corsaro, and J. Streeck. Berlin: Mouton de Gruyter.

———. and J. Streeck. 1986. "Studying Children's Worlds: Methodological Issues." In *Children's Worlds and Children's Language*, edited by J. Cook-Gunperz, W. Corsaro, and J. Streeck. Berlin: Mouton de Gruyter.

Cottle, T. 1972. *Black Children, White Dreams*. Boston: Little, Brown.

———. 1973. "The Life Study: On Mutual Recognition and the Subjective Inquiry." *Urban Life and Culture* 2:344-360.

Crowe, C. 1981. *Fast Times at Ridgemont High*. New York: Simon & Schuster.

Cusick, P. A. 1973. *Inside High School*. New York: Holt, Rinehart & Winston.

Damon, W. 1977. *The Social World of the Child*. San Francisco: Jossey-Bass.

Davis, K. L. 1940. "The Sociology of Parent-Youth Conflict." *American Sociological Review* 5:523-535.

Dawe, H. C. 1934. "An Analysis of Two Hundred Quarrels of Preschool Children." *Child Development* 5:139-157.

Denzin, N. K. 1977. *Childhood Socialization*. San Francisco: Jossey-Bass.

Eder, D. 1985. "The Cycle of Popularity: Interpersonal Relations Among Female Adolescents." *Sociology of Education* 58:154-165.

Edgerton, R. B. 1984. "The Participant Observer Approach to Research in Mental Retardation." *American Journal of Mental Delinquency* 88:498-505.

Everhart, R. 1983. *Reading, Writing and Resistance*. Boston: Routledge & Kegan Paul.

Fine, G. A. 1976. "Obscene Joking Across Cultures." *Journal of Communication* 26:134-139.

———. 1977. "Social Components of Children's Gossip." *Journal of Communication* 27:181-185.

———. 1980. "Cracking Diamonds: Observer Role in Little League Baseball Settings and the Acquisition of Social Competence." In *The Social Experience of Field-Work*, edited by W. Shaffir, A. Turowetz, and R. Stebbins. New York: St. Martin.

———. 1981. "Friends, Impression Management, and Preadolescent Behavior." In *The Development of Children's Friendships*, edited by S. R. Asher and J. M. Gottman. Cambridge: Cambridge University Press.

———. 1983. *Shared Fantasy*. Chicago: University of Chicago Press.

———. 1986a. "The Social Organization of Adolescent Gossip." In *Children's Worlds and Children's Language*, edited by J. Cook-Gumperz, W. A. Corsaro, and J. Streeck. Berlin: Mouton de Gruyter.

———. 1986b. "The Dirty Play of Little Boys." *Society* 24:63-67.

———. 1987. *With the Boys*. Chicago: University of Chicago Press.

——— and B. Glassner. 1979. "Participant Observation with Children: Promises and Problems." *Urban Life* 8:153-174.

Fine, G. A. and S. Kleinman. 1979. "Rethinking Subculture: An Interactionist Analysis." *American Journal of Sociology* 85:1-20.

Freeman, D. 1983. *Margaret Mead and Samoa*. Cambridge, MA: Harvard University Press.

Furfey, P. H. 1927. *The Gang Age*. New York: Macmillan.

Gallagher, A. 1964. *Plainville: Twenty Years After*. New York: Columbia University Press.

Geer, B. 1970. "Studying a College." In *Pathways to Data*, edited by R. W. Haberstein. Chicago: Aldine.

Giallombardo, R. 1974. *The Social World of Imprisoned Girls*. New York: John Wiley.

Glaser, Barney and Anselm Strauss. 1967. *The Discovery of Grounded Theory*. Chicago: Aldine.

Glassner, B. 1976. "Kid Society." *Urban Education* 11:5-22.

Goffman, E. 1961. *Asylums*. Garden City, NY: Doubleday.

———. 1974. *Frame Analysis*. Cambridge, MA: Harvard University Press.

Gold, R. L. 1958. "Roles in Sociological Field Observations." *Social Forces* 36:217-223.

Goode, D. A. 1986. "Kids, Culture and Innocents." *Human Studies* 9:83-106.

Goodwin, M. H. 1980. "He-Said-She-Said: Formal Cultural Procedures for the Construction of a Gossip Dispute Activity." *American Ethnologist* 7:674-695.

———. 1982. "Processes of Dispute Management Among Urban Black Children." *American Ethnologist* 9:76-96.

Gordon, Wayne. 1957. *The Social System of the High School*. Glencoe, IL: Free Press.

Greeley, A. and J. Casey. 1963. "An Upper Middle Class Deviant Gang." *American Catholic Sociological Review* 24:33-41.

Gregory, J. 1984. "The Myth of the Male Ethnographer and the Woman's World." *American Anthropologist* 86:316-327.

Hall, S. and T. Jefferson. 1976. *Resistance Through Rituals*. London: Hutchinson.

Harris, T. 1978. "Telephone Pranks: A Thriving Pastime." *Journal of Popular Culture* 12:138-145.

Henry, J. 1963. *Culture Against Man*. New York: Random House.

Hollingshead, A. B. 1975. *Elmtown's Youth and Elmtown Revisited*. New York: John Wiley.

Horan, R. 1987. "The End of Halloween." Paper presented at the Association for the Study of Play Annual Meeting, Montreal, Canada, March 26-28.

Horowitz, R. 1983. *Honor and the American Dream*. New Brunswick: Rutgers University Press.

———. 1986. "Remaining an Outsider: Membership as a Threat to Research Rapport." *Urban Life* 14:409-430.

Hughes, L. 1983. "Beyond the Rules of the Game: Why Are Rooie Rules Nice?" In *The World of Play*, edited by F. Manning. West Point, NY: Leisure Press.

Inciardi, J. A. 1984. "Little Girls and Sex: A Glimpse at the World of the 'Baby Pro.'" *Deviant Behavior* 5:71-78.

82

Jackson, B. 1987. *Fieldwork*. Urbana: University of Illinois Press.

Jenkins, R. 1983. *Lads, Citizens and Ordinary Kids*. London: Routledge & Kegan Paul.

Johnson, J. M. 1975. *Doing Field Research*. New York: Free Press.

Jorgenson, M. 1984. "A Social-Interactional Analysis of Phone Pranks." *Western Folklore* 43:104-116.

Kett, J. 1977. *Rites of Passage*. New York: Basic Books.

Knapp, M. and H. Knapp. 1976. *One Potato, Two Potato . . .: The Secret Education of American Children*. New York: Norton.

Kohl, H. 1967. *36 Children*. New York: New American Library.

Kozol, J. 1967. *Death at an Early Age*. Boston: Houghton-Mifflin.

Langer, D. 1985. "Children's Legal Rights as Research Subjects." *Journal of the American Academy of Child Psychiatry* 24:653-662.

Liebow, E. 1967. *Tally's Corner*. Boston: Little, Brown.

Llewellyn, M. 1980. "Studying Girls at School: The Implications of Confusion." In *Schooling for Women's Work*, edited by R. Deem. London: Routledge & Kegan Paul.

Lofland, J. 1976. *Doing Social Life: The Qualitative Study of Human Interaction in Natural Settings*. New York: John Wiley.

Lowney, J. 1984. "The Role of a Nonparticipant Observer in Drug Abuse Field Research." *Adolescence* 19:425-434.

MacKay, R. 1973. "Conceptions of Children and Models of Socialization." In *Childhood and Socialization*, edited by H. P. Dreitzel. New York: Macmillan.

Mandell, N. 1984. "Children's Negotiation of Meaning." *Symbolic Interaction* 7:191-211.

———. 1986. "Peer Interaction in Day Care Settings: Implications for Social Cognition." In *Sociological Studies in Child Development*. Vol. 1, edited by P. Adler and P. Adler. Greenwich, CT: JAI Press.

———. 1988. "The Least-Adult Role in Studying Children." *Journal of Contemporary Ethnography* 16:433-467.

Marsh, Peter, Elizabeth Rosser, and Rom Harre. 1978. *The Rules of Disorder*. London: Routledge & Kegan Paul.

Martinson, Floyd M. 1981. "Preadolescent Sexuality: Latent or Manifest?" Pp. 83-93 in *Children and Sex*, edited by Larry L. Constantine and Floyd M. Martinson. Boston: Little, Brown.

Maynard, D. W. 1985. "How Children Start Arguments." *Language in Society* 14:1-30.

McCosh, S. 1976. *Children's Humour*. London: Granada.

Mead, M. 1928. *Coming of Age in Samoa*. New York: Morrow.

Mechling, J. 1984. "Patois and Paradox in a Boy Scout Treasure Hunt." *Journal of American Folklore* 97:24-42.

Mungham, G. and Pearson, G., eds. 1976. *Working Class Youth Culture*. London: Routledge & Kegan Paul.

Murphy, M. D. 1985. "Brief Communication." *Human Organization* 44:132-137.

Opie, P. and I. Opie. 1959. *The Lore and Language of Schoolchildren*. New York: Oxford University Press.

Owen, D. 1981. *High School*. New York: Viking.

Parker, W. C. 1984. "Interviewing Children: Problems and Promise." *Journal of Negro Education* 53:18-28.

Parsons, T. L. 1942. "Age and Sex in the Social Structure of the United States." *American Sociological Review* 7:604-616.

Patrick, James. 1973. *A Glasgow Gang Observed*. London: Eyre Methuen.

Peshkin, A. 1984. "Odd Man Out: The Participant Observer in an Absolutist Setting." *Sociology of Education* 57:254-264.

Piaget, J. 1962 (1932). *The Moral Judgment of the Child.* New York: Collier.

Polansky, N., W. Freeman, M. Horowitz, L. Irwin, N. Papania, D. Rapaport, and F. Whaley. 1949. "Problems of Interpersonal Relations in Groups." *Human Relations* 2:281-291.

Polgar, S. K. 1976. "The Social Context of Games: Or When Is Play Not Play?" *Sociology of Education* 49:265-271.

Polsky, H. 1962. *Cottage Six.* New York: John Wiley.

Polsky, N. 1967. *Hustlers, Beats and Others.* Garden City, NY: Doubleday.

Redl, F. 1966. *When We Deal with Children.* New York: Free Press.

Richmond, G. 1973. *The Micro-Society School.* New York: Harper & Row.

Schatzman, L. and A. L. Strauss. 1973. *Field Research: Strategies for a Natural Sociology.* Englewood Cliffs, NJ: Prentice-Hall.

Scheff, T. 1966. *Being Mentally Ill.* Chicago: Aldine.

Schofield, J. W. 1981. *Black and White in School.* New York: Praeger.

Shaw, C. 1930. *The Jack Roller.* Chicago: University of Chicago Press.

Sherif, M., O. J. Harvey, B. J. White, W. R. Hood, and C. Sherif. 1961. *Intergroup Conflict and Cooperation: The Robbers Cave Experiment.* Norman: Oklahoma Book Exchange.

Sherif, M. and C. Sherif. 1953. *Groups in Harmony and Tension.* New York: Harper.

Short, J. F., Jr. and F. L. Strodtbeck. 1965. *Group Process and Gang Delinquency.* Chicago: University of Chicago Press.

Silvers, R. J. 1976. "Discovering Children's Culture." *Interchange* 6:47-52.

———. 1983. "On the Other Side of Silence." *Human Studies* 6:91-108.

Simons, E. R. 1980. "The Slumber Party as Folk Ritual: An Analysis of the Informal Sex Education of Preadolescents." M.A. thesis (Folklore), University of California, Berkeley.

Sluckin, A. 1981. *Growing Up in the Playground.* London: Routledge & Kegan Paul.

Speier, Matthew. 1976. "The Adult Ideological Viewpoint in Studies of Childhood." Pp. 168-186 in *Rethinking Childhood,* edited by Arlene Skolnick. Boston: Little, Brown.

Spradley, J. P. 1980. *Participant Observation.* New York: Holt, Rinehart & Winston.

St. J. Neil, S. R. 1976. "Aggressive and Non-Aggressive Fighting in Twelve- to Thirteen-Year-Old Pre-Adolescent Boys." *Journal of Child Psychology and Psychiatry* 17:213-220.

Stone, J. L. and J. Church. 1968. *Childhood and Adolescence.* 2nd edition. New York: Random House.

Sullivan, H. S. 1953. *The Interpersonal Theory of Psychiatry.* New York: Norton.

Sutton-Smith, B. 1981. *A History of Children's Play.* Philadelphia: University of Pennsylvania Press.

Tammivaara, J. and D. Scott Enright. 1986. "On Eliciting Information: Dialogues with Child Informants." *Anthropology and Education Quarterly* 17:218-238.

Taylor, S. and R. Bogdan. 1984. *Introduction to Qualitative Research Methods.* New York: John Wiley.

Thorne, B. and Z. Luria. 1986. "Sexuality and Gender in Children's Daily Worlds." *Social Problems* 33:176-190.

Thrasher, F. 1927. *The Gang.* Chicago: University of Chicago Press.

84

Tornabene, L. 1967. *I Passed as a Teenager*. New York: Simon & Schuster.

Turner, I. 1972. *Cinderella Dressed in Yella*. New York: Taplinger.

Vaz, E. W. 1982. *The Professionalization of Young Hockey Players*. Lincoln: University of Nebraska Press.

Vidich, A. J. and J. Bensman. 1964. "The Springdale Case: Academic Bureaucrats and Sensitive Townspeople." In *Reflections on Community Studies*, edited by A. J. Vidich, J. Bensman, and M. R. Stein. New York: John Wiley.

Virtanen, L. 1978. *Children's Lore*. Helsinki: Finnish Literature Society.

Voigt, D. 1974. *A Little League Journal*. Bowling Green, OH: Popular Press.

Waksler, F. C. 1986. "Studying Children: Phenomenological Insights." *Human Studies* 9:71-92.

Wax, R. H. 1971. *Doing Fieldwork*. Chicago: University of Chicago Press.

Whiting, B. B. and J. W. Whiting. 1975. *Children of Six Cultures*. Cambridge, MA: Harvard University Press.

Whyte, W. F. 1955. *Street Corner Society*. Chicago: University of Chicago Press.

Willis, P. 1981. *Learning to Labor*. New York: Columbia University Press.

Wolcott, H. 1983. "Adequate Schools and Inadequate Education: The Life History of a Sneaky Kid." *Anthropology and Education Quarterly* 14:3-32.

Yablonsky, L. 1962. *The Violent Gang*. New York: Macmillan.

———. and J. J. Brower. 1979. *The Little League Game*. New York: Times Books.

ABOUT THE AUTHORS

GARY ALAN FINE is Professor of Sociology at the University of Minnesota, where he has taught since 1976. He has also taught at Boston College, the University of Chicago, Indiana University, the University of Iceland, and the University of Bremen. He has a B.A. from the University of Pennsylvania in psychology and a Ph.D. from Harvard University in social psychology. He is the author of five books and approximately 100 articles on an array of sociological topics, particularly the sociology of culture, social psychology, and qualitative methods. He is the author of *Shared Fantasy: Role Playing Games as Social Worlds* (University of Chicago Press, 1983), *Talking Sociology* (Allyn & Bacon, 1985), and *With the Boys: Little League Baseball and Preadolescent Culture* (University of Chicago Press, 1987). His current interest is in the sociology of aesthetics, which he is exploring through an ethnographic investigation of four restaurants in the Twin Cities metropolitan area. He and his wife Susan have two sons, Todd, age 8, and Peter, age 5.

KENT L. SANDSTROM is currently a graduate student in sociology at the University of Minnesota. He has worked with children for many years in a variety of professional and volunteer capacities. Most recently, he has been employed as a Crisis Intervention Counselor at a shelter for abused and neglected children and as an Area Coordinator of a Big Brothers and Sisters Agency. He has also been actively involved in promoting community education and intervention efforts designed to address the harmful consequences that both alcoholism and physical abuse can have upon the daily lives and self-conceptions of children. His present research interests are in the identity transformations and relationship problems that are experienced by persons with AIDS or AIDS-related infections. He and his wife Vicki have two sons, Nathaniel, age 8, and Philip, age 6.

NOTES

NOTES

NOTES